[redacted]

THE COURT AND FREE-LANCE REPORTER PROFESSION

Recent Titles from Quorum Books

A Problem-Finding Approach to Effective Corporate Planning
Robert J. Thierauf

Managing Risk in Mortgage Portfolios
Alex O. Williams

Evaluating Employee Training Programs: A Research-Based Guide for Human Resources Managers
Elizabeth M. Hawthorne

Current Budgeting Practices in U.S. Industry: The State of the Art
Srinivasan Umapathy

Developing Negotiation Skills in Sales Personnel: A Guide to Price Realization for Sales Managers and Sales Trainers
David A. Stumm

Training in the Automated Office: A Decision-Maker's Guide to Systems Planning and Implementation
Randy J. Goldfield

The Strategist CEO: How Visionary Executives Build Organizations
Michel Robert

America's Future in Toxic Waste Management: Lessons from Europe
Bruce W. Piasecki and Gary A. Davis

Telecommunications Management for the Data Processing Executive: A Decision-Maker's Guide to Systems Planning and Implementation
Milburn D. Smith III

The Political Economy of International Debt: What, Who, How Much, and Why?
Michel Henri Bouchet

Multinational Risk Assessment and Management: Strategies for Investment and Marketing Decisions
Wenlee Ting

Staffing the Contemporary Organization: A Guide to Planning, Recruiting, and Selecting for Human Resource Professionals
Donald L. Caruth, Robert M. Noe III, and R. Wayne Mondy

THE COURT AND FREE-LANCE REPORTER PROFESSION

Improved Management Strategies

DAVID J. SAARI

Foreword by ERVIN G. GROSS

QUORUM BOOKS
New York • Westport, Connecticut • London

Library of Congress Cataloging-in-Publication Data

Saari, David J.
The court and free-lance reporter profession.

Bibliography: p.
Includes index.
1. Law reporters—United States. I. Title.
KF8805.S23 1988 347.73'16 87–13093
347.30716
ISBN 0–89930–234–3 (lib. bdg. : alk. paper)

British Library Cataloguing in Publication Data is available.

Library of Congress Catalog Card Number: 87–13093
ISBN: 0–89930–234–3

First Published in 1988 by Quorum Books

Greenwood Press, Inc.
88 Post Road West, Westport, Connecticut 06881

Printed in the United States of America

The paper used in this book complies with the Permanent Paper Standard issued by the National Information Standards Organization (Z39.48–1984).

10 9 8 7 6 5 4 3 2 1

Copyright Acknowledgment

To Martha with love

Contents

Foreword

It has been my pleasure to work with Professor David J. Saari as a member of the Certified Managing Reporters Institute faculty for several years. With his background as a court administrator and educator he was the ideal choice to design and structure the Institute. Since one of the goals of the Certified Managing Reporter Program of the National Shorthand Reporter Association is to assist court administrators and judges in the management of court reporters, his background in the judicial field brought the required insight to the program.

This book will serve as a useful text for CMR's who have completed the program. In addition, it will have real value to all those in the court community who deal with court reporters. It will be of interest not only to reporters who manage other reporters, but also to individual reporters who simply want to learn how to better manage their own individual courtroom or free-lance practice.

The author offers an enlightening and comprehensive analysis of the origin and history of the reporting profession, and documents the efforts of the profession to become a cooperative part of the judicial team. He sets out in detail for the reader how the CMR embraces organizational theory and practices, personnel management, and the intelligent and proper use of technology for the benefit of the consumer of reporting services.

The overall value of Professor Saari's effort is greatly enhanced by his judicious use of experienced and prominent reporters in the field who recognize the necessity of the profession's responsibility to the public.

I heartily recommend the use of the book to anyone who is interested in the efficiency of the reporting system within the entire judicial structure and within the legal profession and legal community.

ERVIN G. GROSS
Freelance Principal
Minneapolis, Minnesota
President, National Shorthand Reporter
Association, 1981–1982
Chairman, Certified Managing Reporter
Committee, National Shorthand
Reporters Association, 1987

Acknowledgments

As the author of this book I owe a long list of thanks to reporters—both past and present. The spirit that animates this book is one of appreciation for a reporter profession that I have gotten to know much better in the last few years. I hope this book helps reporters and the legal community of lawyers, judges and court administrators to understand one another better by concentrating on the important points about reporters—a human service profession no less than the legal profession. For a very long time I have thought that a better public discussion of reporters is absolutely vital to improve relationships among the professions. If this book contributes to the goal of improving relationships, it will have served a useful purpose.

The contributors are owed a special thanks for their writing efforts in the order appearing in the book: Eileen Hyatt, Karen Carney, Regis Taylor, Marguerite Stebbins, Linda Valentino, Jay Suddreth (president of the National Shorthand Reporters Association, 1986–1987), John (Jack) Byers and Erving Gross (president of NSRA, 1981). Special thanks are due to Frank Nelson (former president of NSRA), Herbert Avram, Harry Foster, Ben Rogner (editor of *NSR* magazine), Jerry Miller and William Oliver (president-elect, NSRA, 1987–1988). Their help in reviewing drafts was very important to me. Also, the splendid cooperation of Karen Jacoby and others of the NSRA Staff and the help of Charles Hagee, executive director of NSRA are without any parallel in my past experience. A special thanks is due to three research and academic friends: Professor Leonard Sayles, Columbia University Graduate School of Business; Geoff Gallas, research director of the National Center for State Courts; and Anne Walker, a reporter and new voice on the linguistical side of reporting.

The certified managing reporter students in the last few years have stimulated me to rethink many of the old ideas about the field. The reporters whose work is mentioned here are due thanks for their work of general value. Their professional contributions last a long time.

For errors and mistakes in the book, I take full responsibility. My hope is that the lasting value of this book will contribute toward greater professional development for reporters.

Introduction

What better way to start a book about court reporters and management than to have managing reporters describe what they do and to explain their actions and thoughts while managing. We are fortunate to have these observations and comments from Colorado, New York, Hawaii, Vermont, and Illinois. Scattered across America in free-lance reporter offices and in official court reporter offices, there are reporters who find themselves deeply involved with management of the reporters in their organizations. Two of the following reports of the reporters are from free-lance firms where the writers are managing their own firms in Colorado and New York. Three are reporters who manage reporters in state trial courts in Hawaii, Vermont, and Illinois. Each of these reporters is very experienced in reporting, and over the years has become knowledgeable about management through the experience of managing in the field of reporting. Four of these accounts to be presented are prepared by reporters who have attended all of the certified managing reporter sessions in 1985 and 1986, and are soon to receive certified managing reporter status in the National Shorthand Reporters Association. There is ample evidence from their writing and experiences to call all of them professionals in two senses—reporter professionals and management professionals. All have risen through the ranks to achieve their current status and achievements. Each writer will be introduced briefly before their views are presented.

Eileen Charles Hyatt, who lives and works in Denver, Colorado, is the principal manager of Hyatt & Associates. In 1986, she was president of the Colorado Shorthand Reporters Association. The material that follows was published in the *National Shorthand Reporter* in May 1986, under the title "Managing a Growing Reporting Firm." This key article stimulated the author of this book to seek similar expressions from others in the field of reporting. The other contributions follow the Hyatt article.

Managing a Growing Reporting Firm
Eileen Charles Hyatt, Denver, Colorado

For every project, every career, every direction we undertake in life, we must have a vision. The vision may change and evolve, but there must be an underlying, guiding, driving vision anchored in the subconscious that moves us along our way.

The vision I have for Hyatt & Associates, Inc., is based on three major goals: quality record product, service to people who need our skills and depend on our integrity, and a feeling of belonging to a professional and mature team of people.

Our reporting firm has evolved since 1968. Up to that time my background in reporting had consisted of a year and a half as an official court reporter and a year and a half of travel. I then decided to try free lancing. After much transition, this office is now composed of 16 full-time reporters, who are considered employees for IRS purposes but who work on the same basis as independent contractors. As a matter of fact, and happily so, our reporters are very independent. I like to work with independent people who enjoy taking responsibility for their own lives, actions, and decisions.

We have six full-time staff people, four part-time professional proofreaders, and one principal—me. I rotate in and out of management, marketing, reporting, and new-product development.

Our offices are located in a renovated duplex just east of downtown Denver. We have a large conference room and our own in-office video equipment. We have been on the Baron system of computer for almost seven years and have recently added Baron's new generation of computers, which gives us instant translation capability. Each reporter has invested in a satellite station in her own home. We have an independent computerized billing system and a third computerized system for word processing. We offer all computerized reporting services that are available in the marketplace.

Weekly staff meetings are held, in which each staff person reviews a weekly report from his or her department. A weekly jobs-in-progress report aids in reporting assignments for the next week and also acts as an organizational tool for the reporters. We are currently developing an inventory-control program that will aid in devising annual budgets. Our commission structure for reporters favors holders of Certificates of Merit, longevity, and high volume. All reporters receive an annual education allowance so that they may attend classes or seminars that they feel will enhance their lives, both professionally and personally.

I appreciate the resources we have available, because of our volume, to invest in personnel, equipment, education, and supplies. We pursue the vision with these tools as we build on data and gather experience every day of our professional lives.

BUILDING QUALITY

Quality starts with hiring the best people, people who are committed to the same standard as yours. Therefore, it's important in the hiring process for the office to express its expectations, to test the applicant, or to use whatever means you have available to ensure the best match between the office and reporter.

Hiring is such an important decision that in most cases it cannot and should not be completed in one interview. The interview process is important, however, because you get to use your perceptions and communication skills. To build a team, you must have people you like to be around and whom you appreciate.

A word to those looking for a position: use the same rule for yourself. Do not put yourself with someone you would not want to take instruction from just because today you want a job. You need to work together for a long time, and it's not worth the effort if you do not like the people you work with.

Test the person you are interviewing. Even if he or she has speed skills, use old Registered Professional Reporter (RPR) tests for language skills. Some reporters have been working a long time with marginal or outdated language skills. Call references, especially if you know the people listed.

Training

People cannot know your expectations and standards unless you convey those to them. Develop a manual. At worst, give them your collection of office memos. These memos, by the way, can become a good basis for developing a manual. Assign a mentor from your reporters, someone the new person joining your team will find available and approachable. Test your new reporters periodically on office procedures, litigation procedures, and language skills.

Procedures

The transcript procedure in our office is as follows: each reporter has her own satellite station in her home. Reading and tranning (translation) of the magnetic tape are done on the main-office computer center. The unedited text is then "flopped out" onto floppy diskettes and proofread line by line in the reporter's home on her own schedule.

In order for this system to work, you need to have self-disciplined reporters. Often people cannot work in their own homes because they are distracted by their personal lives and obligations. These reporters would be better off working in the office, where everything is focused on work. But for reporters who are self-disciplined, this procedure gives them a great deal of freedom.

Once the reporter finishes her line-by-line reading, then on her next office visit she "flops" the material back into the main computer and prints a rough copy. In our office, the translation, flop-out, flop-in, print, and bursting functions are in the process of being turned over to a computer-room manager, to further free the reporters for what only they can do: reporting.

The rough transcript is then submitted to our proofreading department, where our head proofreader assigns each job to one of our staff of professional proofreaders. (Our proofreaders' work is read at random at least once a month to keep a quality check on their performance.)

The corrected rough copy then is returned to the reporter who makes changes, prints a final, and submits the final to the production department with a form that completely identifies all information that department needs for photocopying, delivering, and eventual filing.

The production department is our final check for all obvious oversights. When errors are caught in production, they are corrected, but a form advising of the corrections is returned to the reporter and a copy of it goes in her file. When changes are returned by deponents, the reporter also receives a copy, so she knows what areas of her transcript are being corrected. A copy of the changes goes into the reporter's file. While no reporter likes to receive notices of error, we all would rather know where we need to improve. We are committed to a 100 percent verbatim transcript but recognize all the human and physical barriers obstructing that goal.

At review time, once a year, besides looking at the above forms, we also review the reporter's record for timeliness of delivery, volume, strengths and areas needing attention, goals for the next year, and long-range goals in relation to reporting and other interests. I also use this time with the reporter to get feedback as to how the office is doing, what suggestions she has as to strengths and weaknesses in management.

BUILDING SERVICE

There are two basic concepts I have learned in the course of offering service. Number one, find out what the market wants. What is most important to your client: is it high quality and speedy delivery or fancy covers? Is it the latest technology or good conversation? Or is it all of the above? Whatever it is that you perceive is important, set your standard and be consistent in meeting it. Service and quality are a daily commitment. Do not just assume this commitment is being met; always have management checks.

Number two, do not be afraid of making a mistake. For a long time, I lived in dread that I or others in our firm might make a mistake. That kind of fear takes more of a toll than is necessary. After a number of errors over the years and finding that we were still in business, I realized that more important than the error is the follow-up and correction of the error. Most reasonable business people can accept an occasional error. And if you do whatever is necessary to correct that error, even at a financial loss, you can end up with a stronger client connection than if you had never made the error in the first place. That is part of professionalism.

BUILDING TEAMWORK

This is the most nebulous, most time-consuming, sometimes the most frustrating but also the most rewarding part of business. The areas of quality and service are a matter of setting standards, rules, and procedures—and sticking with them. Teamwork involves your skills in working with people, your patience, your integrity, and your ability to look at yourself.

There are many different styles of management. Which one you choose or evolve into depends on the beliefs and personality of the principal. The style that I feel best builds a feeling of teamwork and belonging is the open-management approach. This calls for sharing management information with your office members and asking them to share their information with you.

How the information is shared is important. How to contribute in a positive, non-threatening, and effective way is part of the learning process. Because you ask for suggestions doesn't mean that they will always be effected. Reasons for decisions, therefore, need to be expressed. Open management is a constant flow of ideas and a commitment to working on communication, without getting bogged down in the rhetoric.

One of our forums for this communication is our monthly breakfast meetings. At these meetings we have had a variety of speakers: attorneys, authors, psychologists, and accountants. Our own people sometimes either organize and run a meeting or give presentations on their own educational experiences. Every third or fourth meeting seems to call for a discussion of new office procedures, changes in language rules or rules of civil procedure and custom. When we discuss reasons that cannot always be properly explained in memos, the new procedures make more sense to people and are more quickly adopted.

When we need to let off steam, either management or the reporters will call for a meeting to confront an issue. Confrontation can be uncomfortable but it is also extremely effective in resolving tensions. Conflict then need not be feared but may be used as a tool for growth.

Most reporting firms have developed from active reporters, so we must pick up our business background along the way by trial and error and education. Trial and error can be a long and painful process, so I would urge all developing businesses to build strong business-education courses into their expense and time budgets.

The most important business class I have taken has been economics. Getting an overview of business and how each of our business units fits into the whole, the theory of supply and demand, constant reinvestment of profits, and particularly the theory of diminishing returns, proved vital to the healthy planning and growth of this firm.

As we build on our awareness of responsibility to each other in the office, eventually we see our responsibility to our profession. We then step out of our own office and interact with our own colleagues, even though they be our competitors. We see how our behavior affects the entire profession as it does within our own office. Therefore, we can make a difference; and it is in our own self-interest to consider the whole, since we are part of it.

And beyond ourselves, on a larger scale, what we do has an effect on the legal community and the economic community. We are important in what we do. Even though we're a small part of a much larger process, if we perform our part well, the whole functions better. How we treat each other along the way is another part of professionalism.

USING VISION

Our vision is expanding. What I see down the road is developing reporters in specialized areas: in medical, waste contamination, oil and gas, aviation, areas particular to each locale. No one reporter can be versed in all the areas of technology that we are called upon to report these days.

When I lose my vision, my main concerns are how much I am getting versus giving, how I may have been slighted. Then I develop stress, make poor judgments, feel anxious and insecure. That's when I have to reach back to my vision and let it take a commanding role. I relate this to speed contestants. Speed contestants do not focus on every word; they almost go into another mode or subconscious zone and let all the established mental synapses take over, and their fingers become a vehicle for what has already been rooted in their minds.

When we use vision, we make good decisions, because we are working from information, experience, and inspiration already in place, built upon over the years. When we focus on the quality, everything else we need will follow.

It is with this vision—and with the people in our office—that I hope to continue to build upon our professionalism, while providing avenues for business growth and space for personal development.

Karen Ann Carney is a partner and manager in a New York City free-lance reporting firm of Ralph Fink & Associates, Inc. She describes the growth and development of her firm and the management aspects of her work in a firm that has grown to a size where corporate form became imperative.

Managing A Free-Lance Concern:
From a Cottage Setting to a Corporate Structure
Karen Ann Carney, New York City, New York

Upon entering and leaving the reporting offices of Ralph Fink & Associates, Inc., located in the financial district of New York City, one views a lithograph in the reception area titled "Chaos and Control." I feel it is appropriately placed, for it epitomizes the plight of a manager, and stands as a reminder to my partners and to me that we must constantly search for ways to maintain equilibrium in a forever changing reporting industry.

By way of background, the firm of Ralph Fink & Associates, Inc. is a well-established, free-lance firm that has been serving the legal community since 1958. It was founded by its senior partner, Ralph Fink, who formerly worked in the United States District Court for the Southern District of New York. I personally joined the firm as a staff reporter in 1970, and attained the position of partner in 1974. Jean Brdey, likewise, joined the firm as a staff reporter in 1973, and obtained the position of partner in 1982. Jeanette Erickson, our fourth partner, joined the firm in 1968 as part of our transcription staff and attained the position of partner in 1984.

It is interesting to note that at the time I entered my profession, the free-lance reporting firms in New York City were basically operating in a cottage setting; that is, their staff consisted of a handful of reporters, and their transcribers, in the main, were what can be termed "at-home typists." This setup necessitated the transcribers either picking up or having delivered to them steno notes, dictated tapes, or both, for transcription, and then the return delivery of the transcribed proceedings to the firms for which services were provided; ergo, wasted time. While in the past this structure served its purpose, during the decade of the 1970s an evolutionary process began to take place in the legal community and the court reporting industry, not only in the microcosm of New York City, but nationally as well. The growth of law firms, due to the litigious society within which we are living, and the time constraints placed on busy litigators by the court system, required a modification of their support services, as well as the reporter profession.

As many reporters can attest to, the requests for daily copy (same-day delivery) and expedited copy (three- to five-day delivery) were fast becoming the norm. It was because of client demands of reporters and the desires of management of free-lance firms to facilitate them, that astute managers began to position their reporter firms in the marketplace by becoming self-contained units, offering an array of services to their present and potential clientele, that is, conference rooms to out-of-town attorneys, and technological services such as videotaping, computer-aided transcription, and its offshoots, litigation support services. They accomplished this by hiring the necessary complement of in-house reporters, transcribers, and backup personnel who shared the same intrinsic values and work ethics as they did; hence, the emergence of the corporate structure for a reporter firm.

Since environment will have an impact upon the corporation's personnel needs and how it is managed, I should explain how this applies to my firm's situation.

THE NEW YORK CITY FREE-LANCE ENVIRONMENT

The private sector of reporting in New York City is unique. It is the only city in the United States where a large part of its free-lance reporters belong to a union. The Federation of Shorthand Reporters (union) represents individual reporters whose services are used by principal reporters (owners of free-lance firms) who are signatories to a three-year contract. What has evolved out of this union environment is an almost superimposed organizational structure under which principal reporters and Federation Reporters now function.

Principal Reporters

The following describes a principal reporter's responsibilities:

1. They lease/own and pay for the office space and equipment needs (typewriters, computers used for bookkeeping, word processing and computer-aided transcription, video equipment, xeroxing machines, paper supplies, postage, and so on) of their organizations.
2. They hire, train, and pay the requisite number of hourly/salaried staff (office managers, receptionists, copy room, clerical and bookkeeping personnel).
3. They hire, train, and pay video operators, and also the staff used in the transcription process (notereaders/Stenorette operators for the traditional method of transcription, or scopists/text editors for the automated method "CAT").
4. They have an in-house staff of free-lance reporters (federation members) who they assign to report proceedings. (It should be noted that if principal reporters cannot cover an assignment with their existing staff reporters, they can obtain the services of a federation reporter by calling the union headquarters, and are required to do so before using a non-federation member.)
5. They compensate the federation reporter on a per page basis for transcribed pages (regular, expedited, daily delivery) or one-half the per page rate for untranscribed proceedings, plus attendance fee, or a minimum-fee basis (where applicable) "in full" every two weeks, regardless of whether or not the firm has collected from its clientele.

Federation Reporters

The following describes a federation reporter's responsibilities:

1. Federation reporters are for the most part attached to one reporting firm from which they rent desk space, and thereby are guaranteed an assignment from that firm (if one exists on the calendar), or they may place their name on the union list that principal reporters use to fill an open assignment.
2. After reporting proceedings, they submit steno notes, along with the necessary glossary, to be transcribed by the firm's notereaders/Stenorette operators, or submit notes via Steno RAM or magnetic tapes, if the firm is using "CAT."
3. They pay for their stenographic machines/CAT writers, steno paper, initial CAT dictionaries, and other supplies necessary for the taking of the verbatim record.
4. Once the particular case is transcribed, they proofread the hard copy of the transcript, indicating any changes that need to be made, and submit same back to the firm for corrections, copying, collating, delivery, and billing to the client.
5. After the number of pages is determined as a result of final transcript printout, they submit a bill to the reporting firm at the applicable rate.

These, then, are the major differences between principal and federation reporters in New York City.

BEING RECEPTIVE TO CHANGE

As most managers recognize, the needs of an organization and its staff change over the years, and must be reassessed and analyzed by its management where applicable. During the months of October and November 1986, the principal reporters and federation reporters were involved in lengthy negotiations for a new joint agreement. At that time, after much analysis of the issues involved in the negotiations, the partners in my firm made a unanimous decision that our organization would not be a signatory to the ensuing 1986–1989 Joint Agreement. Therefore, our firm, like other free-lance reporting firms in the New York metropolitan area, while maintaining the "independent contractor" status of free-lance reporters (as well as the roles and responsibilities of management and reporters) has set up our individual compensation system for free-lance reporters performing services for our firm. This new system takes into account each individual reporter's work experience and level of expertise.

While any changes undertaken by management involve certain risks, no matter how well thought out and analyzed, changes are fundamental to operating a growing concern in a competitive environment. However, this decision by management was perceived by the majority of our reporters as favorable, and interestingly has attracted to our firm other free-lancers who want to participate in this new management concept, since they view it as more equitable for all concerned.

MANAGING OUR CORPORATE STRUCTURE

As one of the many firms in New York City whose corporate structure still resides, to a certain extent, under the union umbrella just described, our firm's support personnel, equipment needs, and overhead have increased proportionately with the volume in transcripts we produce, and with the demands of our clientele. Rather than having a few reporters and virtually no in-house support personnel, we presently have 15 staff reporters and 19 in-house support personnel. An offshoot of this growth process has been that the roles and responsibilities of management vis-à-vis the organization and its personnel have become more diverse and complex, obviously requiring a consolidation of talents to manage our structure. Therefore, we have found it advantageous to keep abreast of what is happening within the reporting environment in New York City, as well as nationally, by attending and giving seminars. The benefits derived by doing so have been bountiful. It has afforded us an opportunity to develop friendships with fellow reporters over the years, and to gain valuable insight into business principles which we can apply to the running of our free-lance firm.

In our domain, realizing that no one individual can be omnipresent, and that effective management depends on our outside/inside "eyes and ears," as partners we earnestly attempt to keep each other apprised on a daily basis of what we have ascertained to be taking place from our many contacts. We also hold monthly meetings to analyze problems which may have arisen and to develop different strategies. Because of each partner's relative proximity to outside/inside contacts on a day-to-day basis, we divided up our responsibilities, and delegated them where we see appropriate. Ralph, Jean, and I, as owner/reporters, take advantage of our daily contacts with clientele while on reporting assignments in order to assess their needs, to assess the performance of our reporters, to find out what our competition is up to, and then to use this as a marketing tool. Jeanette, on the other hand, is the inside partner, the overseer on a daily basis of our in-house operation. As she says, she wants to "attempt to maintain a balance within the organization, and avoid 'chaotic disruption.' " She, too, passes the framed lithograph.

In-House Support Staff

The in-house support staff of our firm is distributed throughout three departments (front office, computer, and copy room). Each performs essential yet differing functions; therefore, they are together, a sum of the whole. To exemplify this statement, I would like to offer the thoughts of a sampling of our personnel who work with Jeanette. My reason for doing this is a desire to illustrate our own brand of a particular "work ethic" within the confines of, perhaps, a non-typical, free-lance reporter company.

Front Office Personnel

Our front office is the nerve center of our organization. Its personnel consists of a receptionist, an assistant office manager, and bookkeeping staff. The following are a few observations from the staff about what they perceive to be their duties in assisting management. First, our receptionist: "My primary duty is to screen all incoming calls and route them to the proper parties. Other important aspects of my job are to 'book depositions,' and to inform clients of the status of their transcripts; whether they are still being processed, or have already been delivered and may be lost in the shuffle of their mail room. Another important work obligation is to set up, maintain, and expand the files. Part of this function involves the weeding out of obsolete files and the setting-up of a record retention system. It is a job that gives me the greatest ego satisfaction because this is where I can utilize my past experience. One of my other duties, which falls under the category of 'general office work,' is to record our reporters' incoming and outgoing work, which is then given to the transcription staff or to the copy room for duplication and later delivery to clients. Then there are 101 little details, like spot-checking transcripts, keeping abreast of and ordering coffee and office supplies, setting up the conference rooms when depositions are being taken in-house, and the screening of visitors. But when all is said and done, that's what makes my job fascinating." The receptionist serves as a communication hub.

Second, our assistant office manager: "As my job title implies, many of my tasks in the office revolve around assisting management and our receptionist in work overflow. This might entail anything from preparing invoices and the writing of correspondence, or the calming of one of our harried reporters who is hopelessly lost in a borough of Manhattan searching for a supposed deposition, or their respective queuing up for a day off. As the front office is the final depot before the duplication and delivery of transcripts, I spot-check, along with the receptionist, for any oversight in corrections, and pitch in where required. My pet project has been to organize the office."

Cash flow has a tremendous impact on a company's ability to meet its current obligations and strategic plans for future growth. In the past our bookkeeping staff had been invoicing clients manually; therefore, it was a tedious and time-consuming process. However, after much research and analysis, we recently have acquired a computerized accounting package, and are in the process of fully automating our invoicing procedures. Our bookkeeping staff, assisting management in this conversion, all attest to the fact that over a short period of time we have seen a significant increase in the amount of invoicing we can now generate on a daily basis. Other important features of this system are its production of various reports: aging, cash receipts, monthly statements, sales, billing analysis. Now that we have alleviated the burdensome task of invoicing, our bookkeeping staff can spend more time in dealing with a vexing problem to many reporting firms, that is delinquent accounts. On a daily basis they are in contact with clients who are in arrears via reminder notices or phone contact, and have established a credit rating based on a client's past history of payment.

Although management has delegated certain responsibilities to support personnel, one of the many areas where we feel a need to maintain total control is over the scheduling of reporters.

Scheduling of Reporters

One of the many functions of management is to maintain quality control within the organization. It is fundamental to any reporting firm to adopt an effective system of assigning reporters that will work best in the firm's environment. This involves not only knowing your staff's strengths and weaknesses and what they are most proficient at, but also your clientele. Our particular firm has a mixed client base. It encompasses conservative law firms which practice all the facets of corporate law; federal and state agencies, which deal with civil, criminal, and labor law; as well as private institutions that use our services for conference reporting.

It is because of this diverse client base that we have adopted a quasi-rotation system. What this involves is the segmentation of our reporters into two assignment levels: (1) those who have the expertise and experience to handle any assignment, regardless of difficulty, and (2) those who are neophytes, needing guidance and time to develop their skills. However, there is yet a third assignment factor we take into consideration: (3) the personalities and demeanor of our reporters and clients. While I am sure there are individuals who may look askance at this statement, our rationale is quite logical. It is based on the simple premise that there will be, to start off, varying factions confined in one room over a period of hours, and if the personalities and demeanor of your client and reporter are mismatched, it could lead to a high-voltage situation, with the result being a lost client.

Our firm adheres to this assignment system as much as is humanly possible; that is, we are realistic about its limitations due to the nature of the free-lance reporting industry. We realize that there will be occasions when management will be confronted with unforeseen contingencies, such as a job being called in, at the last minute, and the prime reporter being unavailable. These are contingencies we are prepared to meet.

Computer Department

Management must not lose sight of what essential roles the seasoned notereader/typist plays in the delivery of high-quality transcripts, and the training of neophyte reporters. Our transcription staff has, over the years, become proficient in their skills and knows the idiosyncrasies of different reporters' writing styles and the intricacies of transcript preparation. Therefore, they would be the logical choice of individuals to manage and staff a court reporting firm's computer room. Staffing strategy emerged out of trial and error on our firm's part, since we have taken a variety of staffing approaches. These ranged from hiring a person with programming experience (who soon realized that she wanted to further her career in that regard) to hiring student reporters (who were using this position as a stepping stone while developing their skills eventually to enter their chosen profession—court reporting). Because of this past experience management has developed and implemented a different strategy of staffing the computer department. We took one of our notereaders who had proven her loyalty and expertise, and elevated her to a managerial position in the computer department. She now has overall control of the computer department and coordinates work flow with the front office. Our manager observes: "It is my overall objective in managing this department to ensure the accurate and timely preparation and production of a finished transcript. I consider it imperative, since I am charged with this responsibility, to train the transcription/scoping and support staff sufficiently. In furtherance of a smooth operation, it is my goal to maintain a team-oriented atmosphere and to have a staff cross-trained so they can pitch in wherever necessary." This approach has engendered enthusiasm rather than negativism, since, in the words of one of her staff members: "It has added a new dimension to my career."

Copy Room

Each day reporters have an abundance of critical private proprietary information (the verbatim record and exhibits) at their fingertips. One of the many obligations of reporters to the legal community is to maintain strict confidentiality. Therefore, how we as reporters process this private information is of the utmost importance to ourselves and to our clients. Our firm has its own in-house Xeroxing and messenger staff. The manager of this department, who has been with us for eleven years, states: "My responsibilities are to see that the mail, transcripts, and exhibits are processed in an orderly manner. Each day I interact with the front office and computer room in order to find out what tasks have priority, and then put them in motion."

When one considers the process of court reporting, whatever high technology is used, the layers of execution involved finally terminate in the copy room. This department should never be construed by management to be a "backwater," but it is an equal function in the concerted effort to deliver our product "Across the street—around the world." The client's impression of the firm is sealed into the final deliverable product—how it appears—how it is delivered.

Perhaps these thoughts of staff members would go unnoticed by some management hierarchy. However, I view them as a necessary synergism among support personnel, which is a prerequisite to the longevity and future growth of our organization. I feel that my firm has made great strides since its formation because we have been fortunate enough to have a nucleus of reporters and support personnel who have shared the management's philosophy of giving their best for the benefit of their profession and organization.

I realize that the new technological era poses many unanswered questions and potential changes in structure. Our management, as in the past, is willing to meet it with open eyes and ears, and will remain receptive to change. However, we will hold steadfastly to the intrinsic values we have maintained over the years that have allowed us to gain our stature. And should we be asked where our firm stands in this regard, it is "to the right of Wall Street."

Regis Taylor is an experienced reporter and has developed management of reporting in a pioneering manner for the Hawaiian courts, and for courts and private reporting firms in California. He describes and evaluates court reporter management in a public context in one of the most advanced court systems in the United States.

Managing Court Reporters in Hawaiian Courts

Regis Taylor, Official Court Reporter and Supervising Reporter, State Courts of Hawaii, Honolulu, Hawaii

My name is Regis Taylor. I am a supervising court reporter employed by the Judiciary of the State of Hawaii. I have been a court reporter for 25 years, and have managed in both the official and free-lance field. At the present time in the State Courts of Hawaii, I am responsible for a group of 26 official court reporters and four support staff. I want to give you my perception of what my job is, and to tell you how I feel about it.

The court reporter's managing office has direct and active interface with the public, the judges and the Supreme Court. As a judiciary manager I respond to the public's questions, interpret and channel their requests to the proper area, and act as their facilitator in all matters.

My responsibility with judges is to mediate people problems, and to handle union contract restrictions between the court reporters and the system, with ultimate goals of efficiency, reporting excellence, and job satisfaction derived from this responsibility.

My contact with the Supreme Court places the responsibility for system design and performance squarely on my shoulders. I must deliver satisfactory production quotas from the group of reporters each month. To perform this responsibility to the Supreme Court, I must successfully manage the interface between the public, the judges, and my office. This requires a system design that is efficient and that allows me to execute a production plan that will meet the Supreme Court's goal. The aim is to manage a happy, healthy group of court reporters who feel they are making a genuine contribution to system goals both personally and professionally.

The human dynamics of this job begin with a diverse, complex group of professionals who often work under combined pressures that are unreasonable. Next, the time and production of these professionals must be managed by a system design that will meet judiciary goals and keep these professionals happy and healthy. These employees must be managed successfully in a public environment that presents built-in limitations and frustrations which may not be readily apparent, but are nevertheless real. A complex employee group is under pressure with a work environment that changes by design to meet expanding goals in a general atmosphere of fiscal restraint. This is the stage and these are the players.

It is truly difficult to resist the temptation to be only goal oriented, to hustle and squeeze the last drop of energy out of the reporter group every day just for the sake of posting statistics that I know will advance my position in the eyes of those to whom I am responsible. I understand the mechanics of human dynamics with relation to reporter employees. I know that I should be fair, sensitive, perceptive, decisive, available, and efficient. I know that I should not criticize openly and should communicate without anger. Many times I just do not want to do these things as much as I want to concentrate on achieving system goals. That is my personality. I am sure that other managers are more comfortable seeking goals from a human dynamics approach. I am even more certain that none of us possesses a natural balance of the two spheres.

Until I had an opportunity to consider management in an educational setting, it seemed normal for me to consider human dynamics and system goals as mutually exclusive. Today, I constantly seek a blending to achieve my goals. If I have a choice of two solutions to a problem and one involves consideration given to employee relations, I will choose that one. I have developed an appreciation of the strength and health that this blending brings to my group. I fear, however, that I will always be tempted to be goal-oriented.

There are some things I do not like about my job. There is a built-in frustration about public sector management that often causes me to modify a goal or fail to achieve it altogether. An employee's satisfaction and performance are affected by many aspects of organizational life other than my behavior, and many beyond my control. Our environment is affected by the independent action of the legislature, political executives, labor unions, attorneys, and other court operations competing for funds from a limited budget. When less tax money is available for government operations, a condition arises that is known as a freeze or retrenchment. I cannot remember managing when we were not in a retrenchment. In such conditions, management will not consider giving merit or performance salary increases to my group. Are they goal-oriented? What happened to human dynamics? The employees resent being told they work in a merit system environment when it is obvious they do not. I resent representing a management team that tells them that when conditions have changed.

In recent years I have perceived a public attitude of suspicion and mistrust of the judiciary in this country. Too many times the media or some probe identifies a person or a situation that is not as it should be. It is embarrassing and personally uncomfortable for judiciary employees to function in the community during these times. I find it relatively impossible to motivate them. I become depressed. It is obvious to the staff, and I do not care. What a lousy job! We cling together emotionally for a brief time in a normal interpersonal reaction, then time, coupled with the strength and vitality of each individual's personal life, washes away the depression. What a great job!

I would not feel complete in my job environment if I did not have the opportunity to experience the satisfaction of successfully achieving a goal through planning and performance. I perceive myself as a public sector manager with private sector drives. I appreciate the opportunities given me by the judiciary to manage my responsibilities freely within our organizational constraints. Public sector management often is organizationally difficult, but I could not have developed the guts and sense of character I have anywhere else. I have been a respected professional court reporter for 25 years. I am very proud of that. I have been a manager of these systems for 15 years, and I now consider that the greater accomplishment.

Marguerite A. Stebbins manages reporters in a state-wide system of courts. Her extensive reporting experience and several years of service in a state position has given her an unusual perspective on management in the judicial branch of Vermont.

Managing a Court Reporting Program in Vermont

Marguerite A. Stebbins, Managing Court Reporter
State of Vermont Courts, Middlebury, Vermont

In most respects, Vermont's court reporting program probably differs very little from other court reporting programs around the nation. Although organizational structures may vary from state to state, the basic principle remains the same. Reporters work in various branches of the judiciary, and are supervised by one or more superiors. In Vermont, as in other states, this position is called managing court reporter.

What makes the job of managing court reporter in Vermont unique is the fact that the Vermont judicial system lags far behind the rest of the nation in several significant areas. Salaries for court reporters, judges, and other court personnel are among the lowest in the nation, and resources for professional development are virtually nonexistent. An antiquated court system, often riddled with inefficiency, makes the job of a court reporter in Vermont particularly stressful. Although turnover among reporters has been reduced drastically in the past four years, it had reached crisis proportions during the late 1970s.

The most difficult challenge I have faced in my professional career has been maintaining efficiency and morale in a system which is not overly conducive to either. Nevertheless, progress is being made, and the quality of reporters remains high.

HISTORY

In 1982 the position of Managing Court Reporter was created. Until that time the court reporters were scheduled in the various courts by an assignment reporter for District Courts and an assignment reporter for Superior Courts. All other administrative services, as they related to court reporters, were handled by the Court Administrator's Office. There was an extremely high turnover of court reporters, and a general feeling of chaos prevailed regarding Vermont's court reporter system.

MANAGING COURT REPORTER

I was appointed Vermont's first Managing Court Reporter in June 1982 by the Court Administrator. My background had been as a full-time court reporter in Vermont since 1968. This position evolved under the management framework of a new Vermont Judicial Personnel Policy. As Managing Court Reporter I am responsible for Vermont's court reporting services for the judicial branch as well as working in the capacity of a part-time court reporter.

In the early stages of the program a Vermont State Court system Court Reporter's Manual was written and distributed to all official court reporters. A program of objectives, responsibilities, and performance review was developed and approved by all court reporters. The manual and program have resulted in uniform procedures throughout the state. Court reporters now have a written reference outlining their responsibilities within the system.

PROGRAM OVERVIEW

There are 21 full-time permanent court reporters assigned on a monthly basis by the Managing Court Reporter to District and Superior Courts. There are 13 part-time court recorder personnel working in the District Courts recording arraignment sessions, motions, traffic tickets, and small claims hearings. As Managing Court Reporter I supplement this staff with free-lance court reporters as needed.

Routine monthly operations of the system call for court reporters to send time sheets every two weeks to the Court Administrator's payroll division. The time sheets are analyzed and approved by the Managing Court Reporter each month. This differs from some other states where reporters are paid salaries and are not required to submit time sheets. Court clerks mail monthly court scheduling calendars to the Managing Court Reporter by the 15th of the month for reporter or recorder scheduling for the following month. Transcript reports are due from court reporters to the Managing Court Reporter by the 5th of each month for planning and scheduling purposes. Court reporting services schedules are planned and mailed by the Managing Court Reporter to all court reporters, court clerks, the administrative judge, and Director of Trial Court Administration the last week of each month for the upcoming month.

Staff meetings are held periodically in an effort to improve communications as they relate to policies and plans for the judicial branch. Continuing education of court reporters is one of my most pressing priorities. Official court reporters maintain continuing education credits through their membership in both the National and Vermont Shorthand Reporters Associations.

Morale

The feedback received since 1982 in regard to the court reporting program is that morale among the official court reporters has been greatly improved. Most probably this is attributable to the creation of the position of Managing Court Reporter, since now reporters have a supervisor who shares their professional needs and concerns. There is a greater sense of job satisfaction, loyalty, and commitment than in previous years. I prefer an open management system where court reporters feel comfortable in discussing job concerns with me with the expectation that those concerns will be appropriately addressed and resolved to our mutual satisfaction.

Work load

The population of Vermont grew 16.4% from 1975 to 1985. The caseload in the Supreme Court has increased 84% in the past ten years. In that same period of time Superior Court cases have increased by 30% and District Court cases by 86%. These figures alone are evidence of the tremendous demand which has been placed on Vermont court reporters for appellate transcripts. There have been no increases in court reporting staff since 1982. To compound this problem, the budget of the Vermont judiciary is only 2.3% of the total general fund and the prospects for increased funding of the judiciary are bleak.

Day-to-Day Crises

All the planning and thoughtful decision making that goes into a month-to-month assignment calendar for court reporters may be shattered by a telephone call. The name of the game for the Managing Court Reporter is a "contingency plan." It is sometimes difficult at the end of the month to recognize the calendar you mailed at the beginning of the month because of numerous changes at several courts. The court planning a two-week murder trial had a change of plea before the jury drawing. You move your expert court reporter to another court where the court reporter has an appellate backlog or expedited transcript load. Another court reporter calls to request a replacement for one week because of a family emergency. An attorney calls to request an expedited transcript from a court reporter you had planned to assign to a four-day felony case. When you request the reason for expediting, you learn that the attorney's appellate case is being heard that week in Supreme Court, and someone just discovered they were missing a transcript of a hearing which is crucial to the appeal. The Payroll Division of the Court Administrator's Office calls to inform you that one of the court reporters forgot to send a time sheet for the prior two weeks of work. You interrupt your work, look up the schedule, give it by phone, and immediately contact the court reporter to send a time sheet to cover this call. A judge calls to complain about a court reporter or a court reporter calls to complain about a judge. The mail for the day keeps getting pushed to the back of your desk because the telephone is keeping you occupied. The list of interactions with other people in the court system on a daily basis is never ending. There is no question that management of court reporting services is a full-time job. There is no "quick fix" in this type of management system.

FUTURE

The challenge of the managing court reporter is to improve the use of court reporter time, so that appellate cases are not delayed by the unavailability of a transcript. Since Vermont does not provide CAT equipment to its reporters, the processing of appellate transcripts using traditional methods is very time-consuming. A reporter who is not operating at peak efficiency further exacerbates this problem. Although CAT equipment is now used by 13 out of 21 court reporters, its use has been the result of a desire on the part of individual reporters to increase their productivity. The use of court recorders for limited hearings has given time to official court reporters to become proficient on CAT should they desire to purchase their own equipment. I see CAT as our best hope for keeping up with the increase in court volume at a cost savings to clients and taxpayers.

My experience over the past few years as managing court reporter is that Vermont court reporters are committed to their careers. They have accepted the fact that our budgetary constraints have forced the use of limited tape recording in some of the state's courts, and that our court reporting services program in the future will probably consist of a comfortable mix of highly skilled and registered professional reporters, some of whom have already obtained their certificates of merit, and court recording personnel who are also committed to the services they perform. Despite some of the problems that were outlined, I am confident that reporters in Vermont will continue to meet the challenge of providing top quality reporting services at a reasonable cost to the people of the state.

Linda Valentino works in a managerial capacity in one of the largest court systems in the world—in Chicago, Illinois. The evolution of the courts in Chicago and the evolution of the organization and management of court reporters reflects the unique history of Cook County. Management is a most significant subject in this setting.

Managing Reporters in Chicago

Linda Valentino, Assistant Administrator, Municipal Division
Circuit Court of Cook County, Chicago, Illinois

Cook County has one of the largest court systems in the world. The official reporters (about 300) who work in this system are employed by the State of Illinois, but are under the direction of the chief judge of Cook County, who has the authority to hire or fire any reporter. I am one of the administrative staff members of the official court reporters of Cook County.

All "officials," as court reporters in Cook County are called, must first be licensed as a certified shorthand reporter through the Department of Registration and Education of the State of Illinois and must also have passed the officialship test administered by the Supreme Court of the State of Illinois. This assures the public that reporters have the basic skills necessary to report and know about and are bound to follow the rules and regulationsof both agencies—the Supreme Court and the Department of Registration and Education. Salaries and page rates for the officials are regulated by state legislation. In the past ten years the officials have become astute in the political field to assure themselves of salary increases and page-rate increases responsive to inflation and other costs. The organizations of officials have hired a lobbyist who alerts the officials to any legislation that may affect court reporters, and the lobbyist develops and lobbies for legislation on behalf of the officials.

For Cook County, the state of Illinois employs approximately 300 reporters and 20 support clerical staff members. Official reporters are not unionized. The official court reporters' chain of command is depicted in this diagram:

	Administrator	
	Deputy Administrator	
Assistant Administrator		Assistant Administrator
Supervisors		Supervisors
Assistant Supervisors		Assistant Supervisors

The administrator answers directly both to the Chief Judge's Office of the Circuit Court of Cook County, and, since reporters are employees of the State of Illinois, reporters also fall under the management of the Administrative Office of the State Supreme Court. These dual lines of management control have not always been clearly delineated in advance, and often have caused some confusion and delay in accomplishing numerous tasks. The administrator of the official court reporters is chief executive officer. It is his responsibility to make many management decisions in the office. The deputy administrator is the administrator's right-hand man, helps in decision making, and is in charge of officials in the absence of the administrator. The two assistant administrators are the buffer zone between the supervisory personnel and the administrative personnel. Their responsibility is to evaluate each problem or request and to make the recommendations to the administrator and deputy administrator. The supervisors oversee the day-to-day operations of a court division, making sure that all assignments of reporters within that division are completed and that everything runs smoothly. The assistant supervisor assists the supervisor in the daily routines and takes over the day-to-day operations in the supervisor's absence. Now that I have tremendously oversimplified each job description, you now have an idea of the basic responsibility each job entails, and how it relates to others in the chain of command in the Office of Official Court Reporters.

My job title is assistant administrator of the municipal division. Approximately one-half of the official reporters of Cook County fall under the jurisdiction of the municipal division. Ten supervisory personnel assist me. The municipal division is broken down further into six municipal districts, which are designated Municipal 1 through Municipal 6. After official reporters are hired, they are sent to the Education and Training Department for orientation, a training period, and skill evaluation. At the end of this period the reporter is assigned to either the Municipal Division, which is my bailiwick, or the Law Department, the other assistant's jurisdiction. On a day-to-day basis I do not come into contact with the reporters. They are directed to me only if there is a disciplinary problem, special request, complaint, transfer request, or any other extraordinary problem that the supervisor does not have authority to handle. These experiences are the most rewarding for me personally. I enjoy the personal contact, and it gives me an opportunity to see how the districts are working as perceived by the official reporter. This can be very enlightening. In these instances, being aware of office policies, I counsel the reporters on appropriate procedures or interpret the rules and regulations for them. I then make recommendations to the administrator and deputy administrator for their decision. Most of the time my recommendations are adopted; this gives me great job satisfaction because I always try to be as fair as possible when submitting management recommendations.

The most challenging aspect of my position is dealing with other agencies. Everyone is looking out for number one, be it themselves or their agency. Adept negotiation skills are a necessity, an honorable reputation is a must, and, obviously, a congenial personality is like frosting on the cake. It certainly does not hurt negotiations. The deputy administrator has all these attributes, and I have called on him more than once to help me out of tough negotiation situations with other agencies.

Almost everyone will agree that the reporting staff is an integral part of the judicial system. However, we are seldom consulted even on matters that affect us or our work. Unlike other judicial employees in Cook County, we are *not* elected officials (such as the sheriff's and clerk's offices), nor do we hold professional degrees (such as the judges, public defenders, and the state's attorneys). Of course, I feel that reporters have a professional stature, perform a professional job, and are paid a professional wage for their efforts. I have learned that educating the other agencies about the true nature of court reporting has opened many previously closed doors. Some have been closed, in part, by the cavalier attitude of a few reporters who desire to work as individuals rather than become part of a team. They wish to disappear into their own little fiefdoms created long ago. These reporters do not realize that the judicial system has become "big business," and it must be treated as such. In fact, the public expects more from public offices because their tax dollars fund its operation.

Along with tremendous growth and reorganization has come the birth of the Office of Official Court Reporters. It must deal with other judicial agencies and is often the key communication link between individual reporters and the judiciary. The office has been working closely with the Executive Officer of the Chief Judge's Office for the Circuit Court of Cook County. This association has closed the communication gap created by years of autonomous thinking by individual reporters. The lines of communication are now open. Managing reporters understand what court managers want, and they understand how we can provide it. The Executive Officer has helped us to create a pilot program computerizing many of the daily tasks of the supervisors that presently dominate two-thirds of their working time. The Executive Officer has recommended that a management seminar be created by the National Shorthand Reporters Association for all supervisory and administrative personnel. What significant progress we have made in understanding one another!

The Office of Official Court Reporters has grown in size, technology, education, and management. Even though at times it seems that problems never stop cropping up and communication never stops breaking down, I would not trade my job for any other. While perfection is impossible to achieve, the people in the Cook County judicial system are progressive, intelligent, and hardworking. It is a large, diverse, and exciting system, just the same as the city and county it is a part of—the City of Chicago and County of Cook. I am proud to be a part of it.

FROM PRACTICE TO THEORY

The world of reporting and world of management are now overlapping one another everywhere in the United States. These five excellent and vivid descriptions of management activity in the field of reporting lead us into a wide range of further questions that will become grist for the analytical mill of this book. The question of the professionalism of the reporting field itself is asserted by Valentino, and several others, especially Taylor, indicates that management activity is professional in nature. The issues of professionalism need to be sorted out and analyzed at some length. These tasks start in Chapter 1.

The management of reporters—scheduling their daily activities in the public and private agencies—is not a simple job. It is the hard work of supervision—endlessly variable and, at times, thankless. Every one of the five reporters noted the personnel end of the work. In Chapter 3 personnel issues are examined in greater depth. The financial end of managing and marketing of reporter services in a competitive environment are two other significant aspects of management in the private firms. Both Carney and Hyatt reflect on this. But notice that the public sector managers—Taylor, Stebbins, and Valentino—run headlong into many similar problems in Illinois, Hawaii, and Vermont state courts. Chapters 4 and 5 explore the financial and marketing dimensions of managing in the court reporter field. Finally, technology—any and all technology—is used in reporting. Managers do need to know about technology—CAT, audio recording, stenotype, television. From a manager's perspective the world of technology is not limited to what a particular reporter can do to report. The question of group behavior is paramount—to serve the judiciary and the legal profession and other public and private clients most effectively and efficiently. Chapter 6 examines the technology issues in greater depth.

These five practical managers and business people give us plenty of food for thought about practical management issues. Here management finds its justification in our thinking—it is a practical form of thinking that is applied broadly to business affairs. Art museums, farms, and universities are managed. Businesses—large and small—are managed. Professional groups of architects, dentists, lawyers, physicians and reporters, as well,—are managed. What ties together management thinking and action across such diversity is organizational theory, a more abstract level of thinking about some types of human behavior in groups. In Chapter 2, the basic ideas of organizational theory are described and applied to the field of court reporter management. But we have just seen organizational theory emerge in the statements of the five reporters who manage every day. Taylor remarked that systems management and human relations need *not* fight with one another, or contradict or cancel one another, although he struggles with the issue continually. Carney writes about the chaos and central equilibrium point in that complex environment of reporting in New York City. Valentino described the bureaucracy in the Chicago courts, using a chart of various positions. Hyatt used role theory when she wrote: "People cannot know your expectations and standards unless you convey these to them." And Stebbins described the name of the game in Vermont—a contingency plan for scheduling and assigning reporters based upon expected, or predictable, uncertainty in managing. Management that is based upon organizational theory is worthy of study and capable of being studied. That is the reason for the certified managing reporter program of the National Association of Shorthand Reporters and that is the reason for Chapter 2 of this book.

Let us move next into a very difficult area of analysis to take a deeper look at the field of reporting. These ideas need to be explored to make certain that management ideas are applied properly and soundly in the reporter field. The question is: what is the nature of the reporting profession?

1

The Nature of the Reporter Profession and Business: Its Evolution and Direction of Development

INTRODUCTION

What do official and private free-lance reporters do when they work? The answers to this question depend upon how deeply the question is probed. Some probing is offered in Anthony N. Morphy's booklet, *How to Be a Court Reporter* (Morphy 1980). Mary H. Knapp offers views of reporting in *The Complete Court Reporter's Handbook* (Knapp 1984). Knapp covers the elements of a career, courtroom and deposition procedures, producing transcripts, official reporting, and aspects of private reporting. In *Reporter Technology*, the experienced authors offer another view stressing computer-aided transcription, word processing, and videotape information (Block, Farrey, Jacoby, Logan, Loser and Smith-Agren 1986). These works begin to explore the nature of the reporter's job, but either they do not examine the topics covered here, or they differ considerably in treatment of the topic. This book departs from the material just cited in a variety of ways that should become clearer as the chapter unfolds.

At the outset, be alert to the fact that the word "reporter" is ambiguous. The word "reporter" refers to television reporters, newspaper reporters, and reporters for other news media. Exclude this group of journalists/communication types from your thinking. The word "reporter" reminds one of a secretary, too. Some court reporters are titled "reporter-secretary," serving dual functions of personal secretary and official reporter for judges, but it is the reporter side of official court reporters that is the focus of this book, not the secretary side. Most reporters are *not* official court reporters; most reporters are free-lance reporters who are self-employed or who are in contractual or direct employment by a reporting firm. Most reporters have their own clients. The reporter who is the subject of this book centers much of his or her work in the legal field, but some of these reporters also report conventions or other large gatherings of a wide variety of groups, where there is little of a legal nature. Others report closed-captioning for the television industry. Finally, reporters in the United States usually are *not* interpreters of foreign languages heard in courts or in other legal proceedings. Reporters report what the interpreter (another specialist) says in English in the formal setting while under oath. All of these distinctions are important to understanding the role of reporters who are the subject of this book.

The nature of the reporter's job—at least part of it—is esoteric. Reporters use a strange symbolism—shorthand—and they use unusual equipment (not typewriters) called stenotype machines that are stroked with their fingers to record speech by means of phonograms. By way of explanation, a phonogram is a character or symbol used to represent a word, syllable, or phoneme. And a phoneme is a member of a set of the smallest units of speech that serves to distinguish one utterance from another in a language or dialect. Since shorthand and stenography are based upon phonetically abbreviated communication, the links among phonetics (scientific study of speech sounds of a language) and phonemes (sound units), and phonography (system of shorthand based on sound) and phonology (science of speech sounds) are rather complex relationships. Phonemics is a branch of linguistic analysis that consists of a study of phonemes. Phonology is a study of the sounds of speech that is embedded in a larger field of linguistics. To expand further, linguistics is the scientific study of human speech including the nature, structure, and modification of language. A branch of philology focuses on historical and comparative linguistics in literature and sheds light on cultural history (Liles 1975, Chomsky 1986). Psycholinguistics is the study of linguistic behavior as conditioning and conditioned by psychological factors, and, finally, sociolinguistics is the scientific study of linguistic behavior as determined or influenced by sociocultural factors. These fields of study are directly relevant to the definition of reporting developed in this chapter (Walker 1985). And, to add to the strangeness of new scientific fields of interest in reporting, reporters today have begun full-scale use of customized computer systems.

Somehow, sitting in courtrooms during trials, sitting in legislatures and administrative hearings, sitting in conventions and other public meetings, and working on depositions in a lawyer's office, reporters "get" what was said, and afterward, they produce a written version of what was said—a transcript of the proceeding. It all seems so simple and straightforward. However, what happens before, during, and after the event to be reported is not at all clear to most people. And the upshot is a verbatim written record of what was said. But is it so deceptively simple? Do we understand what a verbatim record involves?

You have listened to many teachers in school and college, and have tried to capture in writing what they said. On a daily basis you make notes about what other people said—for example, grocery lists, shopping lists, notes at meetings, and so on. You know how difficult it is to write down what another person said, and even the speaker may not remember exactly. The speaker may vary the sentence unintentionally, even if asked to repeat it at the time it is said. For example, when you are lost, think of how often road instructions are difficult to follow, and then you become lost again, even if directions are written. In exasperation, a direction giver may say to you, "Just follow me!" Thus, you are familiar with what reporters do, since you do it, too, but you would rather not be faced with capturing exactly what was said orally because it is a very difficult task at times. University students frequently find note-taking quite complex, and they ask teachers for permission to bring their recording machines into class just to relieve themselves of some of the classroom stress of taking notes. It is safe to conclude that you share insights into a reporter's work, but is equally true that you remain unaware of a vast world of knowledge and activity that surrounds and penetrates the field of reporting. Dispelling some of the strange and unfamiliar notions is an important purpose of this chapter. The process of dispelling is just like peeling an onion. The dry, outside, dead skin is a review of the misconceptions and prejudices about the reporting field which will follow shortly.

Chapter 1 is a prelude to the other chapters of the book, but this chapter is an important foundation to create a permanent, common understanding of what reporters do at work. Obviously, the foundation offered here would be a waste of time if we shared the same understanding of the field of reporting. Since 1964 I have puzzled over some of the questions posed by this chapter, but only now is it clear that the questions and assumptions about reporters deserve further attention, statement, analysis, and reflection. Please bear with me in what is an extended review of the nature of the reporter profession and business. The aim is to see the reporter profession in a new light of understanding and comprehension. One outgrowth of reflection is development of the human service model of reporting described near the end of this chapter.

SOME MISCONCEPTIONS AND PREJUDICES

Perhaps identification of some misconceptions and prejudices about reporters would help to clear the air immediately. This is the superficial layer of thought to strip away. In one way or another all of the following beliefs about reporters are false or, if true, only so under very limited circumstances.

Reporting is nothing but high-grade penmanship or secretarial work; anyone can do it. Reporters are just like a conduit—like a water pipe—through which words flow from the speaker's mouth to the reporter's ear, to the fingertips, to symbols on paper, to written English words and sentences on paper after transcription. Reporters are just computers—merely digital in nature in their mechanical task of reporting. Reporters never experience any significant discretion in making the record. Reporters are, in a legal sense, just like court clerks and sheriffs—mere ministerial (no discretion) officers of the court. Reporters work only in courts. Reporters are mere functionaries—not doing anything very important in the scheme of things legal. It follows that reporters can and should be replaced easily with audio or video equipment. Furthermore, reporting is not a profession—it is just a craft or trade, largely unskilled. Or reporting is just a business. Reporters are an obstinate group, some of whom should be held in contempt of court when they do not meet deadlines for filing transcripts in courts. Reporters are their own worst enemies. Reporters are backward, nonprogressive types of people, clinging to the past. Reporters are overpaid for essentially clerical work. Reporters need little education to do their work. Reporters are now, and will be, completely replaced by machines. Reporters are not needed to run courts—other countries do not use reporters; they have the judge write a summary. Reporting is a dying occupation, a dying profession, if it even is one. There is a shortage of reporters because there is no future for them in the United States.

Those were very powerful indictments of the reporter profession. What a litany of errors about reporters I have heard for more than 20 years. I even believed some errors in the past. I am not arguing, either, that reporters are always ethical, professional, or dedicated—they are not all saints any more than any other professional group.

These assertions about reporters are not exhaustive. Instead they are exhausting emotionally, especially for the thousands of reporters who are out on the job every day. Just how true are some of these assertions? Assessing these assertions is part of the aim of this book. After you have finished the book, go back over these assertions and decide for yourself about their truth or falsity. Let us turn next to the main messages of this book.

MAIN MESSAGES

Message No. 1—Human Service

Reporting is a human service with both professional and business characteristics.

Message No. 2—Professionalizing

Reporting is a human service that is becoming increasingly professionalized from a long-standing set of craftsman's standards of work. There are significant legal, ethical, and policy aspects of the reporter profession deserving a greater understanding.

Message No. 3—Organization

Reporting is a human service that is being organized increasingly from solo practice into a variety of organizational group patterns of service in both the public and private sectors of society.

Message No. 4—Model of Reporting—Human Service

Reporting is a human service that filters oral language, translates it into writing for the legal profession and others, and produces, by law and by agreement, written words and sentences in a form acceptable to the legal profession and to the judicial branch of government, and to many others in government and the private sector of the economy according to variable and consumer-oriented user conditions.

Message No. 5—Technology

Reporting is a human service that is evolving with a multitechnological base of support systems—audio, computers, video, word processing, optical scanning, electronic mail, and others.

Message No. 6—Future

The human service of reporting has nearly a century of current development in the United States and it will be needed in the future as long as human beings need lawyers, courts, legislatures, conventions, and other recorded gatherings.

While you may expect immediate elaboration of each of these main messages, it would be better to consider their explanation to be a function of the balance of this and the following chapters. This chapter follows the order of the main messages. For example, the persistent theme—"reporting is a human service"—is taken up in the very first layer of analysis with special emphasis later as a potential model of reporting. The professionalization processes are described more fully next. The main messages are the fundamental views adopted in this book to explain the nature of the reporting profession. You may wonder, just how fundamental are these perspectives?

MIND, MACHINE AND LANGUAGE

The main messages are based upon an observation that the relationships of mind, machine, and language are grist for many fields of knowledge, and that these relationships are still open to questions from philosophical, scientific, and humanistic perspectives. One tendency that we have as humans was noted by an English psychologist, James Russell, who said: "Whenever mankind has been profoundly baffled by the mind it has tended to erect analogies to the mental functions that reflect its own state of technological development—wax tablets, hydraulic devices, cameras, telephone exchanges and now computers" (Russell 1984, 138). Furthermore, Russell suggests that we try to make the mind intelligible by showing how it is like something else. But he cautions us to avoid this type of analysis and to think instead *that the mind is not like anything else*—that such analogies could well mislead and fail us. However, this is easier said than believed, since mechanical or other analogies are used in this book, but their limits are openly acknowledged. It is important to be aware of the fact that the mind is so complex that in 1981, Charles Hampden-Turner drew at least 60 word-pictorial maps of the mind taken from a wide variety of fields—history, religion, psychology, philosophy, physiology, communication, language, cybernetics, myths, and other fields (Hampden-Turner 1981). Russell argues further that, as language is acquired, thought develops—that we do not have a "language of thought" to acquire our own language in infancy. And, he suggests that it would be a great mistake to regard language as nothing more than a representational and expressive medium; or just as grave a mistake to regard a computer as having human consciousness. Artificial intelligence is seen for what it is—a contrived thing. Human intelligence, by contrast, is natural and powerful to an unknown degree. What has emerged is a computational theory of the artificial intelligence of the mind that Russell indicates was developed by A. M. Turing, M. Minsky, H. Simon, G. A. Miller, J. A. Fodor, and elaborated by Noam Chomsky. Russell disagrees with the validity of the computational theory of the mind (Russell 1984, Chps. 3 and 7). I do not favor the use of computational theories and chemical theories to describe human nature completely, especially to describe the human mind. All are limited in different ways (Hampden-Turner 1981). Richard M. Restak, a physician who recently produced the book *The Brain*, part of the Public Broadcasting System (PBS) series, concludes that artificial intelligence devices are unlikely to overpower the human brain because neurons in the brain are wet and alive, as opposed to computers which are dry and dead (Restak 1984, 361–362).

Why should the reporter profession be concerned about the limits of computers and the limits of computer-based technologies such as artificial intelligence? One reason is that reporters now use computers in increasing numbers to produce transcripts and to manage their firms or divisions of courts. That is reason enough for concern. Even for noncomputerized reporters the issues about limits of computers are important to understand, since there are many advocates who claim that the expertise of reporters could be reduced to digital logic and could be displaced soon by machines that use computers and artificial intelligence.

To illustrate this viewpoint, let me use a relevant recent example for reporters. Raymond Kurzweil, who is known for his work on artificial intelligence, mentioned a new product of his firm—the Kurzweil VoiceWriter—during his March 1986 interview in the *New York Times* (Foderaro 1986). In that interview the reporter noted:

> But until recently most of these systems had limited vocabularies, were responsive only to a limited number of voices, required the speaker to pause between words, or had combinations of these faults. Now they are being overcome; the Kurzweil VoiceWriter, for example, *which will be available in the middle of this year*, has a vocabulary of nearly 10,000 words. The vocabularies of most systems now on the market do not exceed several hundred words (Foderaro 1986). (Emphasis added)

A quick check with the company a year later shows that the VoiceWriter product is still being tested but is expected to become available for sale later in 1987. A general purpose artificial intelligence machine of this type in the language field would be a dramatic step, and reporters would probably want to test the product immediately to determine its usefulness to them. The use of both shorthand and voice options would present new input combinations for reporters, and this could well lead to further development for some reporters but potential obsolescence of skills for other reporters. No one knows what the probable impact would be of such a new system.

For those in the field of computers, there seems to be a boundless optimism about the reach of computer technology. Many consider Arthur C. Clarke to be one of the best science fiction authors because he wrote *2001: A Space Odyssey, A Childhood's End* and *Songs of a Distant Planet*. As a futurist in a new book about the year 2019, Clarke sees the future of artificial intelligence this way:

> Artificial intelligence, still in its infancy, will dominate the educational system of 2019. . . . Within a decade, the machines will be able to see, listen, talk in languages ranging from English to Japanese, learn and make judgments. (Clarke 1986, 85)

Clarke and many others are filled with unlimited optimism that certainly adds excitement to the future. But the conduct of the reporter profession can not be based upon optimism alone; it is better to be realistic as well. This takes us to another very important set of viewpoints on the limits of computers and artificial intelligence.

Two leading thinkers in the field of computers and artificial intelligence, both at the University of California at Berkeley, are Hubert L. Dreyfus, a professor of philosophy, and his brother Stuart E. Dreyfus, a professor of industrial engineering and operations research. Since 1964, Hubert Dreyfus has examined in detail the limits of computers and artificial intelligence. He has published books and articles in this field, including a very early paper in December 1965 for the Rand Corporation titled "Alchemy and Artificial Intelligence." His early teaching at the Massachusetts Institute of Technology led, in 1972, to a book titled, *What Computers Can't Do*, (revised by Dreyfus in 1979). In 1986, the brothers coauthored the book that summarizes over two decades of work—*Mind Over Machine, The Power of Human Intuition and Expertise in the Era of the Computer* (Dreyfus and Dreyfus 1986.) During the last two decades both men have given significant time and careful attention to a very complex subject at the leading edge of knowledge development in our society. They have a unique combination of scientific and philosophical backgrounds. To recount in any useful detail the major points in their work would not serve the purposes of this book, which has the modest aim to alert readers to a variety of important viewpoints for further research and study. However, it is important to convey the flavor of their long observations and insights from their latest work.

The conclusion of most significance for reporters is this:

> Despite what you may have read in magazines and newspapers . . . twenty-five years of artificial intelligence research has lived up to very few of its promises and has failed to yield any evidence that it ever will. (Dreyfus and Dreyfus 1986, xi)

This is an extraordinary and condemning indictment of the the field of artificial intelligence by eminently qualified experts. To match this conclusion they state:

> Our bottom line is that computers as reasoning machines can't match human intuition and expertise, so in determining what computers should do we have to contrast their capacities with the more generous gifts possessed by the human mind. (Dreyfus and Dreyfus 1986, xi)

In their most recent book, the Dreyfus brothers explore the subjects of intuition and expertise: how and why these ways of knowing differ completely from the digital logic of the computer. They are *not* concerned with an appropriate use of computers as tools or as automatic data-processing devices. Reporters are now using computers and automatic data-processing devices as tools. Their major concern is enlarging computer use beyond those two spheres into areas of human intuition and professional expertise by displacing both with artificial intelligence. In three fields—defense, management, and education—there is a new and concerted effort to "knowledge engineer" the computer into a role of such magnitude that other foundations for human actions are driven out. This is the very real danger of subjugating ourselves to machines by becoming enslaved in some irreversible manner based upon digital logic only. Putting digital logic in its proper channel, given the optimism of its proponents, is now and has been for the last two decades a difficult task for the Dreyfus brothers. What has this epic struggle of such diverse experts to do with reporters?

In the development of this book, the creation of the new human service model of reporting in this chapter is based explicitly on the following assumptions. First, the human mind is not an information-processing device. The mind is not similar to a computer in any realistic way. The metaphor of the human mind being like a computer is one of the more tragic fallacies being promoted today by science fiction and by some scientists who are indentified by the Dreyfus brothers. Second, reporters need to know that their expertise in many fields of knowledge is based upon native rationality, intuition, and expertise formulated through years of experience in their field. These three significant and different bases of knowledge are unique to them as human beings. Their knowledge, for the most part, is not shareable with others, especially with system designers and programmers for computers. The Dreyfus brothers carefully document the high hopes of the promoters of artificial intelligence, and then they document the sober reality that follows when the promise fails in actuality. Reporters need to keep an eye on the promoters and follow their promises, including those made above, into the real world.

By opening up the field of reporting to such levels of discourse, it is possible now to illustrate more vividly that the human service perspective adopted here is based upon a wider vision of reporter work than mere computational or mechanical efforts of the mind. Central to reporting is the ability to use language. This is one of the most complex of all human functions. In fact, as we progress into the more detailed levels of reporter activity, it is possible to see with greater clarity the nature of the important linguistic and other judgments one makes when moving vast volumes of oral language heard in English into a written form and style—one of the basic tasks of reporters. And other tasks require even more complex judgments in which discretion is a large component of decision making, especially in management choices. Reporters, as a group, exercise significant judgment in every phase of their work, and not much of their work is highly programmable, even though computers can assist them. For example, a recent development of great significance in transcript preparation is called CAT—computer-aided transcription.

QUANTITATIVE MEASURES

From the analyses provided so far in this chapter, one could conclude that a series of quantitative measures would support the idea of a changing nature of the reporter profession. As Arthur M. Schlesinger, Jr., said:

> The last three centuries have seen dazzling revolutions in scientific theory and dazzling advances in the translation of theory into technology. This cumulative increase in the rate of change has been the decisive factor in the making of the modern world. The world has moved faster than ever before, and until recently it has moved fastest of all in the United States. (Schlesinger 1986, 20)

Figure 1
Total Reporter Membership: National Shorthand Reporters Association 1900–1987

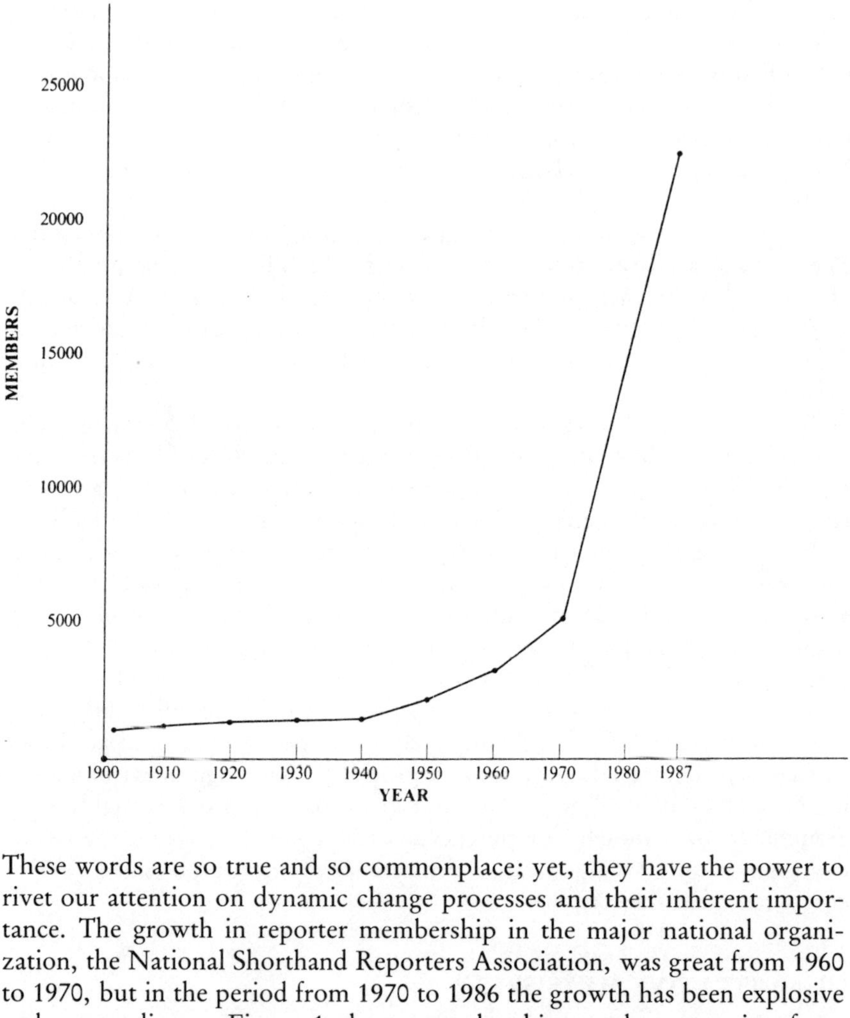

These words are so true and so commonplace; yet, they have the power to rivet our attention on dynamic change processes and their inherent importance. The growth in reporter membership in the major national organization, the National Shorthand Reporters Association, was great from 1960 to 1970, but in the period from 1970 to 1986 the growth has been explosive and extraordinary. Figure 1 shows membership numbers growing from about 5,000 to more than 22,000 in just the last 17 years. Of the 16,000 current professional members, roughly two-thirds are free-lance, the other third is made up of official reporters. Every state is represented, and territories are included. Canada and Jamaica are represented. The geographical spread is complete (NSRA 1986). This is the professional core of reporters in this nation. About 6,000 students of reporting are members of NSRA.

It is important to note that there are other fringe reporter populations not included in this analysis, such as those official audio reporters (in Michigan), stenomask reporters (in North Carolina), audio and video specialists and others who simply do not belong to NSRA but who may belong to a state association of reporters. None of these groups will become part of this analysis, which is confined to the dominant active pen and stenotype reporter group.

State associations are very common, and licensing or certification exists across the nation in some states. State-mandated CSR or Certified Shorthand Reporter status that is recognized by NSRA exists in twelve states: California, Idaho, Illinois, Iowa, Kansas, Nevada, New Hampshire, New Jersey, New York, Oklahoma, Texas, and Utah. It also exists in Canada. Supreme Court-mandated CSR states are Arkansas, Colorado, Hawaii, Louisiana, Michigan, and New Mexico. The last group of states is not recognized by NSRA for reciprocity purposes. Even so, the growth of both the numbers and the certification process is a clear indicator of professional development. A minute presence of de-professional activity exists in a few counties where audio reporting prevails and in a few states where audio reporting is used in rare cases or when no appeal or transcripts arise during legal proceedings.

Free-lance reporter firms exist in most of the metropolitan areas of the nation. These firms may include up to 50 reporters, and they represent a tendency toward group practice in the reporter profession. This same trend toward group practice exists in the legal profession but it is more pronounced in some legal firms with over 750 members (Curran 1986). But reporter firms represent substantial investments in capital to provide space, computers and other modern equipment, and related services. Reporter firms also represent management complexity that will be examined later in this book. The quantitative measures show growth discontinuity in the reporter profession—a fact that should be obvious and expected. This is the changing nature of the reporter profession described so far in this chapter. Let us turn next to the subject of professional processes at work in the reporter profession to see the nature of this occupation in another light, based on sociological literature about professions.

PROFESSIONAL AND BUSINESS DIMENSIONS

The examination of the reporter profession would be incomplete without referring to literature on the professions, which is the object of study of some sociologists. The definitions of a profession are many, but, according to philosopher Alfred North Whitehead, it is generally a vocation or calling whose activities are subject to theoretical analysis and whose activities are modified by theoretical conclusions derived from the analyses (Lynn 1965, v). Teachers, lawyers, and clergy are among the oldest professions defined in such a way. But given the expansive growth of occupations under modern pressure of specialization in the work force, many other occupations have achieved a full professional recognition—military, medicine, engineering, and architecture (Larson 1977). People in other occupations, such as airline pilots and computer experts of all kinds, are in the process of professionalizing or have reached professionalism recently (Vollmer and Mills 1966; Etzioni 1969; Cullen 1978). It is important to note that there are *no* absolute criteria to judge which occupational groups are more professionalized than others (Cullen 1978, 210). As Cullen indicates, "Simply put, a range of occupations exists with some being more professionalized on some selected occupational characteristics" (Cullen 1978, 210). The process of professionalizing is usually associated with modern societies and their drive toward greater rational ordering. For example, in the United States well over 15 million positions are in the professional and technical groups. However, there is evidence that the tendency to professionalize may have ancient origins. For example, the Sumerian priests existed as early as 3000 B.C., Chinese literati in the early Chinese civilizations and courtiers in the European Middle Ages are all evidence of the tendency to professionalize (Cullen 1978, 4).

The reporter professes to know more than others about the making of official and private legal records. This profession licenses, certifies, and registers its members. Groups of reporters join to offer service in a group setting thereby conforming to the medical and legal group practice trend—professionalizing in an organizational setting as opposed to going alone into solo practice. Not every scholar or researcher agrees on the dimensions of a profession, but here is a common list gathered from among 16 leading authorities (Cullen 1978, 15). According to these authorities, a profession:

1. Is organized
2. Involves a complex occupation
3. Has self-employed members
4. Is person-oriented
5. Involves altruistic service
6. Demands long education and training
7. Requires a code of ethics
8. Uses competence testing
9. Licenses its members
10. Offers high income
11. Rewards its members with high prestige

As Cullen noted when composing this list, none of the 11 criteria is critical, but combined, all form a gestalt from which one infers the existence of a profession and a process of professionalization in that occupation. Certainly, an important question is—to what extent are reporters professionalized? Already some evidence has been presented, but let us now focus on these

11 factors to integrate the view of professionalization into a more coherent whole as we explore the nature of reporting.

Professional Characteristics of Reporters

Organization

Given the data offered above describing the explosive growth of the national organization of reporters—NSRA—from 5,000 to 22,000 in 17 years at the national level, there is clear evidence of great organizational ability. My personal observations over several years of NSRA activities at the national level would underscore the attainment of high levels of organization. State and local organizations of reporters are further evidence of organized activity. Professionalism is alive based upon this criteria. Some reporters are unionized in some states—New York for example. Unions of physicians, university professors, and lawyers exist, and they point to de-professional trends in those and in reporter groups.

Complex Occupation

The proof that reporting is a complex occupation rests partly upon the educational programs required to learn the basics of the work. There is also a widespread belief that four to six years of further maturation must occur to reach high professional quality in reporting work. While the base of reporter education is believed to be at least high school, large numbers have some college, some have bachelor's degrees, and a few have even more advanced education. Reporting school specialization follows for a couple of years. More important is the fact that reporting is a lifetime learning occupation. The world that needs to be reported is constantly expanding, and litigation involving it will inevitably be reported by reporters. This chapter, in describing and analyzing what reporters do, contains very complex analytical material and illustrates just how complex reporting has become. The interactions among ears, hands, and brain are some of the most complex activities of human beings.

Self-employed

Most of the reporters in the United States are free-lance within the largest core of professionalized reporters in NSRA. About two-thirds are free-lance, and many of these are self-employed reporters or independent contractors. This compares with about a third of reporters who fall into the official or court category, or are government employed (NSRA 1986). There are 21 states that have government-employed reporters who also do free-lance work. The strong influence of self-employment is a key feature of the reporter profession in both the free-lance and official type of reporting.

Person-oriented

Reporters are experts in the area listening and reporting what they heard. Testing levels at NSRA national meetings over many decades show that reporter accuracy in difficult reporting situations exceeds 97% to 98%. This is a one-on-one personal service for the person speaking as well as for members of the legal profession who retain reporters. Their services are calculated on a page-rate basis, almost on a craft basis, but this may be changing rapidly with CAT technology and the sale of computer floppy or hard discs. The pressure from the insurance industry, varying forms of competitive bidding, and other evidence suggests that group-related service rates are rapidly coming into being in the field of reporting.

Altruistic Service

Just as lawyers provide pro bono work for the poor, reporters are now providing pro bono services for indigent persons in civil and criminal cases. The same motivations prevail in both professions, and programs to nurture and inspire altruistic spirit on the national and local levels are an important part of the reporting profession.

Long Education and Training

The lifetime learning needs of reporters have already been mentioned. Reporter schools are only the beginning of a reporter's education. NSRA has always had a continuing education program on a wide variety of subjects. It has offered non-campus, degree-oriented programs for members. Planning is underway for a full-scale, national program of professional, continuing education courses for reporters that will serve the need for improved learning opportunities. The subjects would include aspects of law, social sciences, linguistics, English, management, humanities, and technology.

Code of Ethics

A national code of ethics will be reviewed later in this chapter. State groups have such codes of ethics. Ethical prescriptions affect reporting in the same way that lawyers and physicians are affected by ethical considerations in their work.

Competence Tests and Licensing

The testing and certification of reporter competence was reviewed previously in this chapter. Compared with the legal profession, this area of professionalization for reporters is not developed adequately, but work is underway to improve this aspect of professionalism. Even video specialists are now certified by NSRA, and soon management specialists will be certified in a program that will be described in much more detail later in this book. In fact, major chapters of this book point to the content covered in the management certification process. Of course, the principal professional certification and licensing is for reporting competence and qualification, and it is this activity that dominates both national and state groups of reporters who exercise lawful authority in the field. There is no doubt that this area is one in which the reporter profession is growing rapidly.

High Income and High Prestige

As with any professional group, there exists a range of incomes in the profession of reporting. Some reporters in the free-lance field and some official reporters who also function as independent court reporters in their private businesses have high incomes and high prestige. They report the most complex litigation and the largest cases involving the litigants who can afford such services. At the other end of the spectrum, reporters new to the profession, reporters who are tied solely to a government salary and rarely receive transcript income, semiretired reporters, and others preparing criminal transcripts for indigents probably fit into a comfortable middle range of incomes comparable to those in other professional groups. The majority of reporters is certainly economically and socially well off.

The close association of reporters with the intimate details of the professional work of lawyers, medical personnel, and business people lends prestige to their work. Every significant social conflict that erupts into some form of executive, legislative, or judicial action of governmental groups or private conflict usually has a reporter present. Those involved in resolving conflict are accorded special significance in the American society. This includes the reporter profession.

After reviewing the criteria of professional status and the professionalizing process in the reporter profession, some conclusions seem reasonable in light of the evidence:

- Reporters are full-fledged professionals.
- Reporters are professionalizing some aspects of their profession to a greater extent than in the past.
- Reporting is a human service occupation located centrally in the highest levels of professions in the United States—law and medicine.

- Reporting is based upon many fields of knowledge, reporting skills take years to master, and improvement is a lifelong learning endeavor.
- Reporting requires ethical and moral actions, and beliefs no less significant than those required of any other profession. Serving the truth is the central ethical and professional calling of reporters. This calling requires independence of the reporter profession.

To conclude this review of the professional and business characteristics of the reporter profession, it is important to know that free-lance reporters manage groups of reporters and support personnel in firms that match law firms or groups of physicians in their organizational complexity. As we will see, profit is one of the goals of marketing; avoiding losses and bankruptcy are others. These business characteristics are very significant to private reporters. Later chapters will explain the business dimensions of reporting in greater depth.

It seems clear enough, now that an analysis has been concluded, that professional and business characteristics are fully developed in the reporter profession. These characteristics settle any question about the basic nature of the reporter profession and its identity as a well-recognized profession on a national basis. The human service model to be developed in this chapter predominates, especially in view of the ethical aspects of reporting. Conversely, a mechanical vision of reporting disappears because it distorts reality about the reporter profession. In addition, the evidence and analysis of the reporter profession support the main messages described at the beginning of this chapter. The main messages convey clear and convincing truths about the nature of the reporter profession. Let us take the analysis directly into legal, policy, and ethical issues of reporting.

LEGAL, ETHICAL, AND POLICY ASPECTS

To continue the exploration of the nature of the reporter profession, there is perhaps no part of that nature more significant than the legal, ethical, and policy importance of reporting. From the historical account of the profession offered later in this chapter one can see the many complex features of the reporting profession. But, that perspective does not convey all that one needs in order to comprehend the work of reporters. What is needed is to revive the basic notion of reporting that is explained thoroughly in the work of Louisell and Pirsig. A brilliant 1953 article by David W. Louisell and Maynard E. Pirsig, both professors of law at that time at the University of Minnesota and the latter a Dean for many years, explains the significance of verbatim recording of legal proceedings in American adjudication (Louisell and Pirsig 1953). The significance is defined for both trial and appellate courts; it rests not only upon ethical and legal reasoning, but illustrates clearly that custom, tradition, and psychological factors bear on the issues of making a record. Even though other nations may rely on summarized court records as opposed to verbatim records, the nature of the records made in the United States is now, and has been, intended to be complete enough to satisfy the most exacting demands for literalness or verbatimness of the legal profession who defend the idea of "verbatim" in a contentious setting of litigation.

As we will see later in this chapter, the reporter's work has been affected in a variety of ways by a mechanical model of reporting in contrast to the human service model developed in this book. The mechanical model of reporting sees the recording activities of reporters as mere appendages to the more important work of others such as judges, lawyers, administrators, witnesses, prosecutors, and defenders. And the mechanical model has no room in it for much that makes reporting a professional activity. For example, why should reporters have a code of ethics? A purely mechanical act of reporting requires no observation, no ethical choices. Why ask reporters to take an oath of office? Why do reporters concern themselves with the values of impartiality, integrity, and fairness in reporting? Why should reporters concern themselves with the need for an accurate and truthful record certified by a professional reporter, especially if the truth-seeking goals are not implicit in the underlying tasks of reporters? The truth of what really happened at a trial is in the hands of a reporter. Why, when audio reporting is developed, do lawyers surround it with certificates of truthfulness and authenticity, and test for competent machine operators and transcribers, requiring oaths of them? These trappings of legal, ethical, and policy considerations in making a record are achieved and sustained with great care taken by professional people and professional attitudes. The evidence is overwhelming that American jurisprudence takes the record-making work of reporters with great seriousness and believes it to be an extraordinary and highly important activity particularly with regard to judicial records and transcripts. As Dean Maynard Pirsig and Professor David Louisell noted in 1953, "The consequences of making verbatim records and of the significance accorded them by Bench and Bar, are many and profound. They go to the philosophic roots of judicial administration in the United States" (Louisell and Pirsig 1953, 33). Every day in trial and appellate courts, the product of reporters is tested by adversaries in depositions and trials as it has been tested every day for much of the history of the nation. Pirsig and Louisell credit the verbatim record prepared by the court reporter for being the "dominant influence in making the appellate process a cornerstone of American adjudication." Given this rationale for a reporter's work, the mechanical model of reporting begins to grow lifeless and pale. Much of the last 25 years of criticism of the reporter profession totally ignores the perspective developed by Pirsig and Louisell.

If anything is obvious, it is that those who advocate video or audio recording as "the answer" to the human profession of reporting, certainly fail to understand basic principles of judicial administration. They overlook the significance of the verbatim record in the balance of power inside the judicial branch and between contending adversaries using the adjudicative process under modern rules of civil and criminal procedures and rules of evidence. These considerations are important legal, ethical, and policy considerations rather than questions related to approach or technique of reporting in which both judges and court administrators have interested themselves for many years, during which time their principal interest has been focused upon economic efficiency, rather than the nature of these more important questions of value.

If modern court management has taught us anything, it has underscored the team nature of the judicial branch in administration (Saari 1982). And, a vital part of the team is the professional court reporter who, too often, is seen as a mechanical appendage, rather than as a central actor of equal legal, ethical, and policy significance to judges, litigating attorneys, witnesses, and others. That point is not comprehended by many people. The values supported by the court reporter to create an independently truthful record are just as important as any other values in adjudication. While the negative and unrealistic mechanical views of reporting do exist, there are three legal aspects of reporting that next deserve attention with more analysis. The first legal aspect addresses the nature of the reporting profession in an adversarial system of legal procedure. The second explores the meaning of a verbatim record. The third exposes the values of a court record using the Louisell-Pirsig rationale and then builds on that rationale.

Adversary System

The adversary system of legal procedure is the basic foundation of Anglo-Saxon jurisprudence. It is also the foundation of the American judicial branches (Abrahams 1986). What is distinctive and worthwhile in the judicial branches of the federal government and the 50 states is a process called adjudication—the opportunity to present evidence and arguments on your behalf, and to be heard by an impartial, neutral, adjudicative judge who has power to rule authoritatively and who is subject to appellate review (Fuller 1981; Summers 1984). On the criminal side, adversariness is premised on a presumption of innocence, proof beyond a reasonable doubt, and the elements of due process supported especially by the Fourth, Fifth, and Sixth Amendments to the United States Constitution. These constitutional rights underlie the very definition of American criminal jurisprudence in both federal and state courts. The civil side of the adversary system requires adjudication—with due process requirements permeating the rules of civil procedure and the rules of evidence. Because notice pleading and practice in the last 40 years have elevated the importance of pretrial discovery of the facts of a lawsuit, the last few decades have seen an explosion in depositions and interrogatories. The depositions are formal legal hearings when questions are asked by lawyers of sworn litigants and witnesses before trial with a court reporter present to make a record of testimony taken during the deposition. One of the important premises of notice pleading is that cases are filed publicly without full knowledge of the facts so that discovery processes can then begin in earnest. In contrast, fact pleading systems require facts to be accurate before being plead in written, public complaints. The search for facts precedes public filing in a fact pleading system. It is assumed and probably true that discovery after notice pleading may well lead many litigants to settlement or to dropping their actions. The basic transition in this century from fact pleading to notice pleading, especially since World War II, has cast reporters into an even more central role in working with the legal profession in deposition activity. Thus, the implications of the change from one type of civil and criminal procedure to another has profound, unforeseen significance for reporters, the bench, and the bar. This is another factor that is ignored frequently in studies of a reporter's work. Notice pleading enhances the role of the reporter with the bar.

Until World War II, the legal profession fought a very high proportion of its legal battles in the courtroom, where the role of the reporter was most obvious to the legal profession and to the public. The older form of fact pleading had an influence on this as well. Since World War II, much of the work of reporters has shifted to the lawyer's office or reporter's office where depositions are taken. In effect, the reporter's relationship to the bar has become enhanced and closer. The relationship with the bench has languished and is more distant especially with reporter pooling. In the more private work setting, the crucial facts of a lawsuit are nailed down in writing in a deposition certified by a reporter to be "the facts" of the lawsuit. As each "factual nail" is driven into the lawsuit, it becomes clear that the transcript of a deposition becomes *the critical document base* for reaching truth and finality, and, ultimately, either trial or settlement. The reporter's deposition work also helps to catch liars—impeaching witnesses who lie during trial with a deposition that destroys their credibility. The work of the reporter is central to the impeachment task. The shift in a reporter's work from trial to pretrial over a long period of time, in an adversary system that uses notice instead of fact pleading, is a fact often overlooked in the review of what reporters do today, compared with their role in the legal system a few decades ago. The significance is that the reporter profession has, to some extent, lost its previously close relationship with the judiciary.

Thus, the American adversary system on both the civil and criminal sides needs a neutral record to make it work. If one contrasts civil law, socialist, and communist court systems and their records, one finds judicial summaries made by judges. The inquisitorial systems of these nations casts the judge into the central role of record keeper as well as judge. In contrast, the adversary system in the United States is premised on an independently created record. The separately made record is most widely adopted in the United States where the judicial branches have achieved an independence from legislative and executive branches, perhaps greater than any other judiciary in the world. The independent record of the reporter sustains and checks judicial independence. In the rest of the world, reporters develop legislative hearings records to a much greater extent than judicial records. The attachment of the legal profession to the reporter profession and their interrelationships with the judicial branch in the United States is central to the unique position of reporters in the United States. It is no accident that the most independent judicial branches in the world exist in the United States. Furthermore, it is no accident that the nature of the reporter's role in creating an independent record is linked to the concept and reality of judicial independence.

We can conclude, then, that the nature of the reporter profession is deeply affected by the nature of the adversary systems, by changes in the rules of civil and criminal procedure, and by changes in the nature of legal practice. The creation of the neutral record is vital in the adversary system. Another potential new source for change in viewing the reporter profession is a reconceptualization of the verbatim record. This is worth examining in more detail.

Verbatim Record

The Conference of State Court Administrators, in its survey of court reporters prepared in June 1984, asked: What constitutes a verbatim record? When is the verbatim record, as opposed to a summarized record, required? (Kotzan 1984, 156–167) The answers are fascinating.

The meaning of the verbatim record is obvious to everyone—correct? Not so. In this survey, many states responded that "verbatim" is self-explanatory. That is the dominant American belief. Other responses to the meaning of a "verbatim record" were more varied: *California*—the reporter must note all omissions in record; *Florida*—no part of the proceedings shall be omitted unless all parties agree and the court approves; *Illinois*—all that is said must be included, without editing or correcting; *Kentucky*—the reporter may not add, delete, correct, or editorialize; *Louisiana*—the testimony must be taken down and transcribed word for word; *Massachusetts*—all that is said during every court proceeding must be recorded. . . . the reporter must accurately transcribe without editing or correcting; *Missouri*—disputes as to correctness of record are to be settled by court; *Nevada*—all testimony, objections, rulings, exceptions, arraignments, pleas, sentences, statements, remarks, oral instructions must be included; *New York*—everything said and meant for the record must be recorded; *North Carolina*—verbatim is defined in a written policy of the Administrative Office of the Courts; and *Puerto Rico*—the summarized record is the rule, and verbatim records are not allowed unless the entire record is attached. Puerto Rico reflects the European civil law orientation toward summarized court records. This wide variance in response to "what we all know" about the meaning of the verbatim record certainly does suggest a need for research. Fortunately, Anne Graffam Walker, a court reporter with many years of experience, completed a doctoral dissertation in 1985 focusing upon this very ambiguous legal area (Walker 1985). Since real and potential ambiguity is central to preparing a verbatim record, it is necessary to examine some of the key points in Walker's dissertation, research, and publications.

Walker states that reporters "are the filters through which language in courts must pass, the ultimate arbiters of the verbatim concept" (Walker 1985, 43). Moving oral language to written text in any process—pen writing, stenotype machines, audio recording transcription, video transcription, computer-aided transcription, or voice-writing transcription—rests on government statutes, court rules and legal customs that define the process, upon English language conventions, and on reporter professional practices. But in all cases the human being is the key. Walker notes that there are problems of accurate representation of legal proceedings, and that transcription standards and conventions concern reporters, lawyers, and judges. Appellate judges, in particular, are impacted when they review trial records. As Louisell and Pirsig noted: ". . . it is not unknown for counsel, faced with a trial judge guilty of prejudicial conduct by attitude, demeanor or tone of voice, to have the reporter note in the record the physical manifestations of such conduct" (Louisell and Pirsig 1953, 34). This point illustrates that more than words in the record are absolutely critical to the definition of a fair trial by an impartial judge.

Walker's research and findings implicitly support the professional nature of reporting, the human service nature of the work, its discretionary aspects, and the objectivity required in the reporter role—even toward the trial judge when the judge fails to be impartial. Recording judicial partiality is difficult. It takes some courage as well. Walker states:

> As the official interpreter of the legal institution's constructs with relation to the proceeding being memorialized, the court reporter acts as a language broker between the oral event and its written representation. And it is his or her concept of "verbatim" which provides the filter through which what one *says* becomes what one *said*. (Walker 1986, 221)

It is enough to note that reporters have a significant professional role in determining the meaning of litigation for trial and appeal purposes. This is the ultimate important finding that emerges from Walker's research. It provides another significant justification to suggest a belief in the human service model of reporting.

Values of Verbatim Records

Having covered the adversary system and vebatim record, the third legal area relates to the values generated by a verbatim transcript of court proceedings. Of course, the qualifications just mentioned above apply to the meanings of verbatimness. Even with these qualified meanings, the Louisell-Pirsig rationale suggests that a verbatim transcript does the following: (1) promotes formality at trial, (2) encourages truthfulness among witnesses, lawyers, and judges, (3) exposes falsehoods, (4) offers permanentness and definiteness to the proceeding, (5) undergirds the full faith and credit clause of the United States Constitution by allowing national recognition of the judicial acts of each state in other states, (6) provides for corrections of errors during trial, and (7) promotes a host of other values—precision, thoroughness, care, restraint, and the discouragement of repetitive behavior. As if these benefits or values were not sufficient, Louisell and Pirsig suggest further benefits from the trial transcript.

On motions for a new trial, a transcript allows more searching reconsideration and, at the same time, reduces judicial arbitrariness and exposes unprofessional judicial and lawyer conduct. The trial transcript allows the losing party at trial to have a record *not written by* a *trial judge* who decided against the losing party, but a record prepared by "the indifferent pen of the ever-recording reporter" (Louisell and Pirsig 1953, 41). The trial judge during trial is psychologically aware that a definite and permanent record is being prepared by a third neutral interest—the court reporter. According to Louisell and Pirsig, the trial judge "stands, in a word, not as the arbitrary master, but almost as the servant, of the record. In this, the verbatim record is an enemy of capriciousness; in this, it serves the ideal of the supremacy of law" (Louisell and Pirsig 1953, 38). Obviously, appellate courts may review trial court decisions more thoroughly and comprehensively with such a record. What is less appreciated is the important fact that if the trial judge is right, the dispositional alternatives of appellate courts are reduced by the trial transcript. Appellate court discretion is limited by the independent record. Most significantly, restraint of the judiciary by the verbatim court record decreases power of the government and usually protects disputing private parties from zealous and overreaching governmental officials. Under the circumstances, the court reporter's role as a responsible actor in trials and appeals is both ultimate and independent. The reporter makes and preserves the record. What more could be said about the important professional nature of the court reporter's work?

The Louisell-Pirsig rationale is rare. It is one of the few intellectually challenging recognitions of the important professional role of court reporters in terms of ultimate values to be protected and promoted. Their reasoning suggests that the verbatim record is faithful to the nature of the proceeding and that parties who are locked in adversary battle acknowledge at least one thing in common—the truth of the trial transcript. And if not, they may litigate about the issue, and a record is made of that. Both the Walker and the Louisell-Pirsig rationale seem to agree that literal word-for-word verbatim transcripts are *not* intended by the legal or judicial professions. What is clearly emerging is a professional decision by lawyers and judges in favor of a *faithful* record based upon professional judgment of a court reporter confined and influenced by educated discretion, custom, and law. All these standards proscribe editing and correcting in general, but allow some leeway to encourage the achievement of a coherent record under professional reporting norms. The faithful record concept is based upon principles of judicial administration coupled with Walker's sociolinguistic work. The concept of a *faithful representation of what was said or experienced at a legal event* is the genuine distillation of the true meaning of the verbatim record based upon research to date. This is what "verbatim" means to those who have given the idea of verbatimness sustained attention and research.

Ethics and Policy

Interestingly, the concept that a faithful record is the same as the verbatim record rests upon moral and logical understanding of truth. The new Code of Professional Conduct of the National Shorthand Reporters Association to govern reporters is filled with the moral prescriptions one would expect to see addressed to human beings as opposed to machines (NSR 1986, 54–56). The reporter's Code of Professional Conduct admonishes reporters to be fair, to be impartial, avoid impropriety, preserve confidentiality, be truthful and accurate, avoid conflicts of interest, and maintain integrity. The reporter is urged to pay attention to his or her own experience and competence in accepting assignments to report, to preserve notes, and to meet deadlines. A host of other legal and educational expectations are also developed. Transcript format guidelines are stated precisely, along with mediation and formal complaint procedures. It is easy to conclude that reporting has very serious ethical implications and that it is usually a crime to tamper with trial records.

So far, then, the legal and ethical bases of reporting offers full support for the main messages stated in this chapter. Recall again that the main messages were premised upon a central belief that reporting is a professional human service. The legal and ethical considerations just reviewed offer further reasons for such a premise. Offering the litigating American public the opportunity to be heard in court under standards of adjudication we have described is an important part of contemporary society. Nothing levels or equalizes litigants in courts with different educational, social, and economic backgrounds more than a faithful verbatim record prepared by a neutral court reporter. The delicate balance of an adversary system is based upon human reporting. Machines would do nothing but disturb the balance and tip control toward the state. State-owned and operated machines present a formidable barrier to challenge the record. In my opinion, it would be a great mistake, from the viewpoint of balanced and checked powers inside the judicial branch—and between the litigating public and the judicial branch itself—to allow state-made records by machines and state transcription services. The potential for abuse is great.

The final points are more general policy considerations that expose some additional facets of the reporter profession. The integrity of trial and appellate proceedings is locked into the integrity of the trial transcript prepared by a reporter. The foundation of the conflict laid out during trial, and eventually represented faithfully in the pages of a trial transcript, is a record of actions taken by counsel and court, witnesses and litigants. The same is true of a file filled with certified depositions: both give assurance to the public of the fairness at trial and the fairness of appeal. Since most of us think of fairness and justice in the same light, reporting is linked intimately to notions of justice being done in our society. If members of the judiciary want to demonstrate their impartiality publicly, they can point to an independently kept trial transcript record to portray the manner in which they fulfilled their responsibilities. If prosecutors hope to show their fairness, it will be on the record. The same advantage applies to defenders in criminal cases who must offer a competent defense. The solid rock of an impartial trial record is the final and unimpeachable basis for ending human conflict in the form of lawsuits. This is the central feature of adjudication, and it is the only place in American society where such high levels of certainty and finality are achieved in a permanent manner. The reporter profession is an integral part of the entire design of the judicial branch and the legal profession.

Another aspect of policy involves court managers whose role in these circumstances seems plain enough, given the importance of professional reporter work. Court managers could develop policies and practices to protect the integrity of the record and the impartiality of the reporter profession. This would undergird the adjudicative process in the courts. Of even more significance is the question: should an independent professional (*an independent private contractor*) keep the official record of trial court proceedings? Or should an employee of the state or an employee of the judge keep such a record? It is easy to see that values of impartiality, neutrality, independence, and integrity can be found just as well in an independent contractor as they can be found in an employee—the legal and medical professions are proof of this. Public reporters who are employees of a government have assured us of their integrity and therefore, are widely used. But private reporters offer identical integrity. The managerial policies toward the reporter profession are important, then, to develop the values inherent in adjudication.

Both the legal profession and the reporting profession have some members who are public employees and some who are independent contractors. The parallel of membership status in these allied professions is significant, since neither professional group is subservient to the state. As if to underscore this fact, the 1984 survey results of the Conference of State Court Administrators found that many reporters who were classified as state or local employees still performed as independent contractors doing private reporting and that in 21 states, free-lance reporters perform significant amounts of the reporting work in courts (Kotzan 1984). This free interchange from private to public arena is the same for lawyers designated by judicial assignment systems to represent indigent accused. Thus, from a national perspective, reporters represent an unusually complex relationship to public authority. This complex relationship is frequently disparaged, especially by public officials who desire to expand their controls and who think the mechanical model of reporting is valid, since they do not believe that reporting is a professional activity. However, it should be clear by now that the human service model of reporting coupled with the legal, ethical, and policy implications just mentioned illustrate rather conclusively that reporting activity, by policy choice, should remain an independent, private activity for the most part—even when it comes to serving the courts of a state or a nation. The limit to the reach of a state or national government with regard to reporters is a basic limit to the power of the judicial branch. This fact is appreciated by some states.

MANAGERIAL VIEWPOINTS

Another perspective developed briefly in this chapter to illustrate the nature of the reporter profession is embedded in the central fact of all professional life in the United States. Most professions are experiencing parallel growth in increased proportions of members practicing in a group, while solo practice is declining. For example, let us examine the latest data about the legal profession.

Although two-thirds of the lawyers in the United States in private practice practiced their profession alone or in association with one or two other lawyers, the legal profession is most significantly moving away from solo practice. The data is very striking, as Table 1 shows.

There are no readily available similar data for the reporter profession. But the growth of groups in the practice of reporting is obvious to every observer of reporters. The monthly professional journal of NSRA, called *NSR*, is filled with the classified advertisements of firms of reporters in almost every major urban center across the United States. Large collectives of reporters work in major urban trial courts. Chicago has over 300 reporters in the Circuit Court operations.

The basic fact of increased organized practice raises management implications for the reporter profession. Several years ago, NSRA recognized the

Table 1
Trends in Legal Practice*

Year	Total No. of Lawyers	No. of Private Practitioners	Percent Solo Practice - All Lawyers	Percent Firm Practice - All Lawyers
1960	285,000	206,000	46	36
1970	355,000	240,000	35	48
1980	542,000	370,000	33	51

*Adapted from Table 6 of Barbara Curran, "American Lawyers in the 1980's: A Profession in Transition," *Law and Society Review* 20, p. 29. Curran does not see as much significance as this author does in the trend toward group practice because of the continued dominance of solo and small-firm practice in the legal profession. Yet, the data illustrate significant shifts toward group practice.

need for management knowledge and training (Gross 1986). The outgrowth is a series of specially designed management seminars called Certified Managing Reporter Modules. The program is known under the acronym CMR. There are five modules of education with the following titles: Organization Theory, Personnel, Finance and Marketing, Technology, and an Internship. These subject areas of the CMR program also define the subject areas of management that form the foundation for the balance of the book.

The years 1984–1986 have been intensive experimental years as these CMR Modules were developed with a growing core of practicing reporters. The work of some of these practitioners who took the CMR program is already explained in the introduction to this book. It will be the principal task of the remaining chapters to explore and explain the types of management problems and solutions that are examined in the CMR modules. Given the nature of the reporter profession described in this chapter, it is more easily understood that reporting, in its best professional sense, is a vital and integral activity associated intimately with the well-being of both the legal profession and the judicial branches of the nation. The cramped vision within the mechanical model of reporting should be identified with its shortcomings and intellectual inadequacies in today's world. The human service model developed next in this chapter is a better and more truthful representation of the nature of the reporter profession in light of available evidence and facts about the reporter profession.

HUMAN DIMENSIONS OF REPORTING

There are at least two contending views of human service in the reporting profession that lie beneath the surface of usual awareness. One view sees reporting to be a mechanical process—a human being is acting exactly like a machine when taking a record using stenotype shorthand by machine or using Pitman or Gregg shorthand with a pen. The second view is diametrically opposed, since it sees reporting activity in very nonmechanical terms. In the second view, reporters are like filters who are straining and sifting human speech through their minds, producing shorthand symbols to signify speech that later becomes translated or transformed into a second version of typed or printed words organized in a style appropriate to human discourse and acceptable to legal conventions and usages. Reporting in this view is basically a translating-transforming activity. The significance of these two disparate views of reporting is of paramount importance to the field of reporting. The significance can be understood by first elaborating a little more on the fundamental nature of each viewpoint.

Defective Mechanical Model

The first view of reporting is the mechanical model. People who believe that reporters are robots or machines also believe that there is some automatic process through which reporters hear and produce symbols on paper. The automatic process suggests that discrete word units disappear into a reporter's ear canal and emerge from the finger tips of the reporter touching stenotype keys or moving a pen on paper. Somehow the word sounds of a speaker are believed to move through the conduit to the reporter's fingers just as water moves through a pipe. The brain is not called into action in any active sense. The second belief associated with the mechanical model is that reporting is merely digital—a numerical process comparable to that of a computers. After all, we now have digital recording of music that sounds faithful to our ears. Would it not also be true that reporters are merely human computers who hear words, mysteriously convert them to numbers or binary symbols comparable to numbers, the way computers do, and finally produce the impression of words on paper? Everyone talks about the "old tapes" playing in the memory of the mind, just like a computer or audio recorder. This theory does sound plausible.

The mechanical model of reporting is comparable to the computational theory of the mind that is powerfully constructed by brilliant researchers who have laid the foundations for the entire computer industry and associated academic fields. The computational or computer analogy is very persuasive, but it points to half-truths in the reporting field. As suggested before, the computational theory of the mind supports the mechanical model of reporting and reinforces the idea that reporting is merely a programmable activity, programmed as a computer is programmed. The mind is a mere listening machine like a tape recorder. Thus, shorthand symbols are just elaborate programs like computer programs. This view of reporting is defective because of the way language is acquired in infancy, the way language is used, the way perception of a familiar face arises in a crowd, the way language is heard, and the way reporters write symbols phonetically and then translate them into English, coupling transformation with human conventions and styles. None of these human activities are programmable except in a highly limited manner. The best example to illustrate the complexity is this: voice recognition research (mechanically moving language from spoken to written form) has struggled for several decades with little success to date, and the prospects are not bright for voice recognition equipment to sweep the field of translation or reporting (Suplee 1986). The computational theory of the mind that undergirds voice recognition research has clear limits that only human beings can transcend. In complex, real time reporting situations, voice writing technology is a relatively weak tool now, although it may play some limited role in the future.

What are the consequences of adopting or assuming that reporting work is mechanical, conduit-like, digital in nature and completely programmable for computers? First, if that view is true, then video and audio recording are sufficient to capture an event and human reporters are truly irrelevant. However, ever since Alaska's successful efforts to record court proceedings in the 1950s just after gaining statehood, we have seen more than 30 years of repeated failures elsewhere to achieve widespread adoption of either video or audio technology with very few exceptions. Alaska is a special place—quiet and remote for recording. And there have been major rejections of audio technology, most recently in New Mexico. The historical review later in this chapter and Chapter 7 will expand on the history of reporting in more detail. What has been repeatedly discovered is that video and audio technology is inadequate for the normal tasks facing reporters every day. Audio technology is in use principally as a listening device in *pretrial* hearings, as a back-up device to a live reporter. For depositions video technology has some value. Where studio-like recording quality is available in a courtroom, and where few transcripts are needed, then audio and video technology has some merit in a few legal proceedings given the strict supervision of trained persons. However, where the conditions are like most normal courtrooms in an older courthouse, and where transcripts are needed for significant adjudicative decisions involving the adversary system, audio and video technology is usually no match for human reporters. The unspoken conclusion that arises from three decades of attempted adoptions is that audio and video technology is insufficient and unacceptable by itself in almost the entire United States. Over the last 30 years the rejection of audio and video equipment has been the position of almost all judges, lawyers, and reporters in the nation. In addition, it is a wise reaction against the mechanical model of reporting and the computational theory of the mind as well. If an innovation has merit, the innovation will be adopted broadly and quickly in the United States (Rogers 1983). This has not been the general national experience with audio or video technology in reporting.

Other consequences flow from the mechanical model or computational view of reporting. Perhaps the worst consequence is an inability to comprehend the professional characteristics of reporting work. This form of blindness to the job characteristics of reporting makes it easy for some to promote the complete substitution of court reporters with mechanical equipment. This promotion is a rare event in American judicial administration history. For example, in 1986, Edward V. Garabedian, then an assistant director in the Administrative Office of the United States Courts, encouraged the use of audio recording equipment in the federal trial courts to suppress the growth of human reporters. "We are simply suppressing the growth [of reporters]. . . . Who is to say what's in store for court reporters? They may be out of a job in 10, 15 years. Engravers are obsolete" (Murphy 1986). This vivid, recent illustration of mechanical modeling or computational thinking at the highest level of the federal court system clearly suggests that misconceptions pervade the administration of court systems. If any court system is housed in older courthouses with high ceilings where it is difficult to hear anything, with a demand for transcripts, and with a real need for human reporters, it is the federal court system. Little adoption of audio or video technology has taken place in the federal system because judges control the process of adoption and they must see the fallacious nature of the mechanical model or computational view of reporting in the federal courts. Equipment failures, "inaudibles" on tapes, and poor transcription service plague that technology.

Another related consequence of the mechanical or computational view is that it has nurtured about 50 years of misunderstanding regarding the nature of reporting. Everyone—judges, lawyers, reporters, and court administrators—has fallen prey to erroneous thinking. Reporters have not marshalled sufficient attention and support for other basic views of reporting. Perhaps the most serious consequence of the mechanical-computational perspective is that it totally ignores principles of judicial administration, laid out so well by Louisell and Pirsig, regarding the values inherent in a verbatim record prepared by a human reporter (Louisell and Pirsig 1953). Over three decades ago, Louisell and Pirsig predicted that human reporters would not be replaced by audio technology and they have been right in their prediction. Previously in this chapter the reasons for their perspective were described and explored in much greater detail. The values highlighted by Louisell and Pirsig have been ignored totally in the discussions of the work of reporters to date.

The unfortunate and misguided views of reporting fostered by the mechanical model are coupled with institutional beliefs of the National Center for State Courts, the Federal Judicial Center and the Administrative Office of the United States Courts. These agencies are still captivated by the mechanical model of reporting. The National Center for State Courts promotes video and audio reporting in the state courts of the nation (National Center for State Courts, June 1986). The federal courts face the same logic from the federal legislative research arm (U.S. Government Accounting Office 1982). The federal courts face a complex promotional activity for audio and video technology (Schleich 1985). These governmental and private agencies are believed to be objective by many judges and their staffs, but in reality, their research and developmental activities in the reporting field are quite remote from objectivity. It is likely that each of these agencies will continue to have a detrimental effect on court reporting services for some years to come, unless, of course, they can begin to comprehend the errors of their mechanical or computational thinking about the reporter profession. The important point to grasp is that it is only under highly limited circumstances that video and audio technology may be useful in reporting, and then only under strict guidelines and totally educated, human supervision with very high quality transcription services. According to NSRA, video and audio equipment alone are not recommended in general jurisdiction courts. In addition, video and audio technologies are simply too old and too slow for transcript work today. The rationale for this logic will be provided later in this chapter where computer use by reporters will be explained. But more importantly, there is another competing model of reporting that is closer to the truth in describing and explaining the real world of reporter activity. This model will be explored next.

Human Service Model

In contrast to the mechanical model of reporting just described, the human service model is a perspective of reporting that is based upon the entire set of human characteristics that reporters bring to the reporting field, coupled with some very limited mechanical or physical analogizing. To begin with, translation is most commonly associated with two languages—something said or written in one language is translated into another language—English to Spanish or vice versa. But translation has another common meaning—that is, a change or conversion to another form or appearance. Oral or spoken English that is changed to written English is a translation process. It is a transformation so basic that it borders on the same act as translation of one language into another.

The change from oral to written English in legal settings (trials, depositions, hearings) is performed by reporters when a transcript is prepared. This is a basic transformational activity (Walker 1985, 1986). However, reporting is *not* paraphrasing, summarizing, or editing, each of which suggests a freer transformation of a legal event to written form. Rather, reporting is a more literal transformation of English from oral to written form, to the extent possible under highly varied circumstances, on a word-by-word, sentence-by-sentence basis as language is spoken and then later as transcribed from shorthand notes into a written form. With computers to assist reporters, this has become an instantaneously achievable process in three or four seconds.

While the translation/transformation activity of reporters is explained using Walker's sociolinguistic work described previously in this chapter, the description of the human perspective of reporting starts with a mechanical type of analogy. The analogy is to the filtering, by the reporter's mind, of the English language spoken in a court or other setting in order to produce shorthand symbols to be later associated with English words in an appropriate transcription style. A reporter acts like a filter—straining away irrelevant speech and other sounds, not reporting some speech where reporting conventions and practices do not require a report, and even reporting some phenomena such as tone of voice and facial expressions when required. Not everything is reported in every setting where reporters work. It never has been. The conventions of the reporter profession and legal profession control the situation. For example, opening statements at trial by counsel may be omitted from the written record in some states. Trial conventions and practices in the local jurisdiction prevail. Thus, filtering is a helpful, human activity guided by professional standards and practices and by important values being established by the nature of the proceeding. Reporting, as Walker points out, could not be done without filtering and transforming the language from oral to written form.

Filtering, as a human activity, means that some spoken words or sounds are not reported. These sounds or words are roughly comparable to the coffee grounds filtered from your coffee every morning; or to the water filtered out of diesel fuel. These are weak analogies, however. Semipermeable membranes in the human body allow some substances to pass through—such as the passage of oxygen molecules into the lungs to be transmitted to the blood stream to oxygenate the blood. These filters keep out dust, debris, smoke, and other harmful atmospheric particles. This sophisticated form of filtering goes on every minute you live, for without it you would be dead. However, when it comes to the mind, the filtering function is somewhat analogous to a trained capacity, a set of routines in memory—illustrated by the way reporters are trained to respond to some sounds and not others. Some words, like grains of wheat, are reported for the record, while the chaff is not intended for the record. Reporting, then, is a dynamic and changeable human process.

The testimony of witnesses, the actual words used and in the same order as spoken in court, is the "literal record" most highly prized and required to achieve the making of a "fact" in a courtroom setting. For example, if the witness says the light was green when she entered the intersection, the light will remain green forever on the trial record if not contradicted. The color green becomes the conclusive fact upon which legal consequences follow. Once the trial ends, no one is in a position to dispute the reported fact. But if the witness clears her throat before speaking, or pauses slightly before pronouncing the word "green," usually these sounds and silences are not reported. However, if the pause is longer than normal speech pauses, the delay may be noted in the record as an indication of hesitation. Then inferences about the veracity of the speaker may be drawn from abnormally long pauses (Walker 1985, 129–134).

The human service perspective is important beyond the recognition that reporting is a translation-transformation activity and that reporting is analogous to filtering. Certain human characteristics are vital for reporting.

Hearing

Reporters, trial judges, and trial lawyers have an astoundingly similar capacity to listen and to hear accurately and completely during legal proceedings of all kinds. It is a trained capacity to give skillfull attention when people speak at high speeds, sometimes expressing themselves very cryptically. What typically develops is a more complete expression of meaning that leads to further questions and answers in an effort to achieve clarity of understanding. It is a fully interactive human process. Active listening by reporters with full human consciousness is unlike a tape recorder listening to sounds and recording those sounds. There can be no comparison of machines to listening, conscious human beings. When it comes to listening—especially listening for meaning in a process just described—nothing surpasses a human reporter to achieve a factual record of the statements made at a proceeding.

Memory

Stored in the mind of a reporter is a changing and vast collection of work-related information: symbols of shorthand, the English language itself, dialects, legal and reporting standards and practices, and more. None of this is static. Memory constantly grows and differentiates under professional discipline. For example, even the reporter's individual dictionary in a computer-aided transcription system starts with one word and continues to grow over time while the reporter's memory grows to upwards of 200,000 or more personal word entries. Thus, the dynamic growing human memory is a unique property of the mind that no mechanical equipment can begin to approximate. Machines do not grow, people do. The growth of memory is vital for transcription work and for comprehension while reporting.

Dexterity

Reporters require great finger dexterity to achieve speeds up to 250 words per minute, or higher, with few errors. This level of speed is slightly over four words a second—a difficult skill to achieve. The human characteristic of finger dexterity is the fastest and most accurate way that the ear, brain, and hands can capture speech and feed it into any storage system, whether note pads or electronic tapes. When speech is too fast for the human comprehension of a professionally experienced reporter, then the reporter slows the proceeding for the sake of an accurate record, with judicial or legal support. In turn, this slower speed assures the judge, jury, trial counsel, and witnesses that the human process of reporting and the trial record remains intelligible for other human beings (Appellate judges) later on, since very often the trial record leads to permanent and final disposition of human rights by a judge.

Knowledge

There are many bases of knowledge in a reporter's mind and files: English language, legal and medical terms, legal practice and procedures, knowledge of practicing bar (person by person), state statutes, and many other sources of knowledge. With continuing education, a reporter's knowledge constantly expands over time.

What can one conclude about the human service model of reporting? If one considers reporting to be a basic set of human activities—listening, writing, reading, and thinking—then the reporter profession cannot be considered mechanical, no matter how much technology is employed by a reporter. If one adds the ideas of translation/transformation and filtering, a better understanding of a reporter's work will be achieved. The human service model is grounded on these realities, yet it contends for a proper position in our minds with the mechanical model that is so defective. The mechanical model is, perhaps, easier to grasp, but it misleads us. Though it is more complex, the human service model is certainly a more reasonable view of reporting reality and should lead to a more balanced perspective of what reporters do at work. The only realistic limits on reporting are human limits, and these are natural limits to hearing, writing, reading, and thinking. Such limits are not to be disparaged in human settings in the way that some complain that reporters experience fatigue and stress while reporting, but machines do not. The fatigue experienced by reporters is also experienced by other speakers and listeners in the setting being reported. The human service perspective stresses the *humane nature* of professional reporting work, kept humane to nurture other values in adjudication such as accuracy, truthfulness, thoroughness, and impartiality. Let us next endeavor to further our understanding of the history of the reporter profession.

HISTORICAL AND INTERNATIONAL PERSPECTIVES

Reporting is a significant activity in the United States today. It is estimated that more than 650,000 appeals transcripts are read by judges in the United

States every year, not to mention the millions of depositions. History tells us that reporting was an important ancient activity at least 2,000 years ago, originating in Europe and the Middle East (Kramer 1959). What can be learned from the past? To provide more background about reporting, a brief historical review is offered here, coupled with a contemporary review of reporting in different legal systems—common law, civil law, socialist law, and others. This comparative treatment is intended to provide a common understanding of the roots of reporting as well as to develop a better idea of the contemporary practice of reporting in different legal systems. For the historical background, I will use material from the National Shorthand Reporters Association prepared in 1976, a Diamond Jubilee convention publication titled, *Celebrating Our Heritage* (National Shorthand Reporters Association 1976). After 75 years of association activity, reporters concluded that their professional history was a vital factor to weave into the comprehensive human perspective of reporting as a full-time occupation. Various reporters prepared the historical account; some material is not designated by a single identifiable author. In the context of the 75th anniversary, the authenticity of these historical accounts seems credible enough for the aims of this book. The NSRA history is not the work of a professional historian—it is professional reporters reporting on themselves. With these limits in mind, let us examine the record developed by reporters of their own history as a field of work. What follows is a summarized version of a much longer historical record: *Celebrating Our Heritage.*

Historical Chronology of Reporting

Cicero's secretary, Marcus Tullus Tiro, in 63 B.C., reported speeches of the famous Roman statesman, orator, and writer using wax covered tablets and a metal stylus. The method of abbreviation consisted of shorthand abbreviation of well-known words and omissions of words easily supplied by memory or by context. The ampersand ("&") is the only sign that remains from one of the first shorthand systems. The first abbreviated writing system in English was published in 1180 by a monk named John of Tilbury. Vertical lines differentiated by short lateral strokes formed this early system. This first period of development in England was followed by a period which remains unknown to reporters. But, in the late 1500s, the first practical systems of shorthand published in the English language were developed by Timothie Bright. In 1602 John Wilks published the first shorthand alphabet in his *Art of Stenography.* By 1620, Thomas Shelton developed a system of shorthand used by a famous English diarist, Samuel Pepys. After Pepys' death, his diary had to be transcribed before it could become suitable for publication. A growing use of shorthand is clearly evident in England.

In 1772 official governmental recognition of shorthand in England occurred when Thomas Gurney was appointed to the first post of shorthand writer in the British government. Eventually, both Houses of Parliament used Gurney's system. A significant English writer, Charles Dickens, used Gurney's system when he was a Hansard Reporter in the British Parliament.

Pitman

By 1837, the year that Queen Victoria ascended the English throne, Isaac Pitman (1813–1897) developed a shorthand system that achieved world-wide recognition. It is so effective a technique that it is still used today. During the NSRA, 1976 Diamond Jubilee Celebration it was noted:

> In all of the diamond-studded history of the National Shorthand Reporters Association, no shorthand nugget can successfully preempt the particular pride of place which the Pitman system of shorthand enjoys: It was there in the reporting from the beginning; and after seventy-five years Pitman is still there, even though much diminished in use. (NSRA 1976, 19)

Samuel A. Fitz-Henley estimated that 95% of NSRA members in the United States in the early 1900s used the system of shorthand invented in England by Pitman. This system spawned at least a dozen variations with speeds of 240–280 words a minute in the United States.

In 1837, Isaac Pitman, who studied and used an earlier system called Taylor's shorthand, published his *Stenographic Soundhand* in English. This was the first truly phonetic system of shorthand. A second edition is titled *Phonography, or Writing by Sound, Being also a New and Improved System.* Pitman revised his system making at least 12 numbered editions before he died in 1897 at the age of 84. The Centenary Edition was published in 1913 and the New Era Version, in 1922. Pitman's work was so influential and important that Queen Victoria of England knighted him. Pitman's self-improvements over many editions plus the variations developed by others were a creative contribution to mankind's use of language. By 1976, Pitman reporters still occupied prominent reporting positions in Congress, the courts, and in free-lance firms in the United States. The former British territories of Canada, Australia, New Zealand, Malaya, Hong Kong, India, Pakistan, the West Indies, and parts of Africa adopted Pitman systems and, in Great Britain, about 2 million people used the Pitman system. Moveover, a quarter of a million begin the study of Pitman shorthand every year.

The global reach of Pitman shorthand is seen in the adaptation of Pitman's system to 30 other languages, including Spanish, French, Welsh, Swahili, Afrikaans, Malay, Hindu, Portugese, and Sinhola. Worldwide adaptability is a significant feature of the Pitman system. Fitz-Henley observes that a study of Pitman systems inevitably results in the writer having a far wider and varied knowledge of the language than before. In addition, the use of shorthand fits into the lives of business people, professional writers, judges, trial lawyers, scholars, students, and many others. By 1972, "Pitman Shorterhand" and "Pitman 2000" were developed to continue this saga of stenography. Fitz-Henley views Pitman shorthand as a personal tool—not limited by machines or environment—with great flexibility and versatility for global use. But even with these desirable traits, other systems of shorthand have developed.

Gregg

The Gregg system of shorthand was invented by John Robert Gregg in 1888. Gregg was born in 1867 in Ireland, where he was trained to use the Taylor shorthand system. He then mastered the Pitman system and finally developed his "Light-Line Phonography." By 1893, when the first edition of Gregg Shorthand was published, Gregg was living in the United States. From 1893 until about 1925, when major shorthand speed contests were won by Gregg shorthanders, his system enjoyed widespread success across the nation and in England. Honored by Bryant-Stratton college in 1929, Boston University in 1930, and later by Rider College, Gregg was widely accepted because of his shorthand system. By 1947, the year of Gregg's death, his system was being taught in more than 20,000 schools and was being used by over 2 million stenographers. NSRA estimated that more than 20 million people across the globe used Gregg systems. Like Pitman before him, Gregg found his systems adaptable to foreign languages.

Both Pitman and Gregg were extraordinarily creative in the field of shorthand written by pen on paper. The history just recounted conclusively establishes their significance. But creative genius in shorthand was inevitably influenced by the creation of typewriters and other comparable machines, leading to the development of stenographic machines used widely in reporting today.

Stenotype System

From the time of the Civil War in the United States until the end of World War II (1868–1945), there were at least 46 identifiable inventors who brought their machine-based shorthand systems for patenting in the United States. Some machines were associated with a foreign language use: a French Palantype machine in 1939; or later, a Russian CTM–2 and a Japanese Sokutaipn. Vast global experimentation was underway, but a few major events dramatically influenced the evolution of keyboard design, machine construction, and the present state of the art of machine stenography. Let us review these events.

The father of the stenotype machine is Miles W. Bartholomew, an official court reporter and a native of Belleville, Illinois. In 1879, he patented the first American shorthand machine. The first model of this device had five needle points that were used to punch holes which recorded speech in a symbolic manner. It used continuous paper in strips about a half-inch wide. In 1882, Bartholomew improved on the system, but his invention was not a financial success even though some schools began using his machine.

Following this very first effort, George Kerr Anderson patented a very different keyboard in 1897. Instead of a letter-at-a-time (or stroke) his was a word-at-a-time (or stroke) system. The keyboards used letters that occur most frequently in English, and there was *not* a common striking point as in a typewriter. Characters were printed across a two-inch-wide tape of paper in continuous strip form, and each character had its own position on the paper. Eight keys on the left, eight similar keys on the right, and four keys for the thumbs was the keyboard pattern. His system was the precursor to the stenotype machinery in wide use today. However, Anderson's commercial venture failed due to poor marketing.

Ward Stone Ireland

Ward Stone Ireland was an inventor who made the greatest contribution to machine shorthand. Born in 1883 in New Jersey, Ireland moved to Maryland to study shorthand at Western Maryland College. During a variety of reporting positions he held, including that as an official reporter for the Panama Canal Commission, Ireland began to develop his significant idea—to reduce or eliminate awkward reaching for keys not directly under the fingers by stroking a word at a time. This concept is called ergonomics or human engineering today, but at that time it was a strikingly new and useful idea. The initial development of the keyboard concept was completed in 1910 when Ireland patented a practical keyboard. Its weight, at first, was 54 pounds but was later reduced to 31 then to 11.5 pounds. This invention eventually led to the creation of Stenograph machine number four, with manufacturing beginning in Owensboro, Kentucky, in 1911. In three months 3,000 machines were sold. By 1913, the company was named the Stenotype company and moved to Indiana. Then, in 1914, a remarkable event took place.

The 1914 National Speed Contest

On August 26, 1914, in Atlantic City, New Jersey, 9 machine shorthanders (15–19 years old) were pitted against 30 seasoned court and convention reporters who used Pitman or Gregg written shorthand. This peculiar test of machine shorthand proved that all nine machine stenotype operators became qualified at 150 words a minute. In two events, machine operators won: (1) at 200 words a minute (straight matter) Fanny Schoenfeld won with 99.30% accuracy, and (2) at 220 words a minute Clem Boling won with 97.37% accuracy. At 280 words a minute (court testimony), Nathan

Behrin, a Pitman writer and experienced court reporter, finished first. But two machine shorthand writers qualified in the 280 word-a-minute event with 97.37 and 95.37% accuracy. This contest in 1914 led to a curious result. Contests were discontinued until the early 1920s, and then only handwriters were involved while machine shorthand writers were excluded. By 1952, machine shorthand writers were allowed to compete in speed writing contests once again. But in 1918 the Stenotype Company, through misfortunes related to World War I, collapsed financially.

Ireland began a new machine company, but it collapsed even with five new patents. Ireland then moved on to other fields and finally died in 1956. However, remnants of the Stenotype Company lived on in various ways until 1927, when the LaSalle Extension University purchased rights in the existing firm. From LaSalle there came another vigorous rebirth of machine shorthand, but the Great Depression of 1929 stopped rapid development once again. By 1937, M. H. Wright formed a company to manufacture and sell an improved machine—the Stenograph. Educational materials from LaSalle were incorporated into the marketing of this machine. The Stenograph was lighter, quieter, and easier to operate. It had a one-way, self-inking ribbon with longer ribbon life, and a better clutch system. At a result, the Stenograph met with success and 2,500 machines were ordered. Supplies and textbooks were updated. But, with the onset of World War II, the Stenograph had to find its way, as it did, into military usefulness.

After World War II, business for machine shorthand grew rapidly as veterans took advantage of G.I. classroom benefits and machine sales soared. From 1940–1975 other modifications to improve efficiency were introduced. The result was the basic, evolved stenotype machine conceived in bits and pieces by many different inventors. In 1956, Wright died, but this time the Stenograph Corporation lived on and does to this day. Machine stenotype shorthand has a secure place in the reporting world today.

There was a further logical development brewing in the 1950s and 1960s that eventually blossomed in the 1980s: computer-aided transcription. Ironically, the entire creative history thus far related dealt almost exclusively with the input side of the reporting equation—how fast and how accurately can one person hear and write down (by pen or by machine) what another person is saying. What followed was an extraordinary period of development: 1960 to 1985.

Computer-Aided Transcription

It is easiest to see the historical transitions from the perspective of the significant reporter who reported the Lindberg kidnaping trial in 1935. The "first Official Stenotype Reporter to serve the District Courts of the United States" was Walter W. Heironimus who reported for the United States District Court in Newark, New Jersey. The year was 1923. A Gregg shorthand reporter for many years, Heironimus learned from the famous 1914 NSRA speed contest, where pen met machine, that stenotype machines were powerful. He said, "After some seven or eight years of unremitting shorthand practice I had reached a ceiling which I easily surpassed after only two years or so of spare time practice on the machine. Why wasn't I able to reach the same speed with shorthand. . . . Obviously, it's the machine that makes the difference—the tool, fulfilling and servicing its purpose or function just like any other tool: to accomplish more with less effort" (NSRA 1976, 41) During his interview, Heironimus foresaw the advent of another technological breakthrough. He said:

> Note-reading transcribers have for years operated routinely and efficiently with stenotype notes, thus speeding up volume transcript delivery; and the emergence now of computerized transcription, apparently just around the corner, would seem to afford a service not adaptable to manual shorthand notes. (NSRA 1976, 41)

The corner about to be turned in 1976 took a few more years to reach a new phase in machine reporting. But this time the output side—transcription—was the major focal point of modern computer technology which has pretty much taken for granted the stenotype input device which was developed more than 100 years ago but was recently modernized in the sweep of a computer revolution.

The CAT Developments—1960 to 1987

Computers did not jump into the lives of reporters. As is typical of any innovative process, there is an expected slow, evolutionary process worth noting. Although CAT or computer assisted transcription is widely used today, in the 1950s, the glimmerings of a computer age about to dawn were barely visible. The advent of large government and commercial computers was rubbing shoulders with reporters in courthouses and business, but direct court reporter applications were nonexistent. In 1964, at the New York World's Fair, IBM exhibited a machine translation system that remained a noncommercial project. The project involved the translation of the Russian language into English. A prototype of a CAT system was developed by IBM during 1963. Herbert Avram worked with the IBM translation equipment while in the service of the federal government in the Washington, D.C. area. Upon retirement, he began to see commercial possibilities in the reporting field. In December, 1968, he formed Stenocomp Company and began to use adapted Stenograph reporter machines for input devices. His company developed and began to market computer software for use on a large, mainframe computer. Avram's experience taught him that anything connected with language was a complex subject; therefore, he began working with reporter Frank O. Nelson of Santa Barbara, California.

These pioneering efforts began around 1970, when Nelson used the first CAT equipment and employed long-distance transcontinental data transmission from California to Washington, D.C. Nelson demonstrated the use of the equipment in New York City, and it appeared that it would be widely accepted. Some years later, Nelson became president of NSRA. But a large computer, the IBM 360/370, was required at the beginning of CAT. This expensive feature made its use by individuals prohibitive. Thus the service bureau concept of sharing costs widely was tried and met some acceptance. From 1969 to 1972, Stenocomp Company worked on the system further, optimizing translation software, broadening lexicographic coverage of its general dictionary, and testing it in various locations. In 1973, Stenocomp became a publicly owned company with hundreds of thousands of dollars invested in research and development. It began to license its equipment and systems. A significant development followed.

In May 1975, Stenocomp contracted with the Philadelphia Court of Common Pleas to allow its equipment and programs to be used on an experimental basis. The federal government Law Enforcement Assistance Administration (LEAA) put $90,000 into the project, while $75,000 came from local Philadelphia sources. The National Center for State Courts was also involved. Some 25,000 pages of transcript were produced on the Stenocomp system during the experiment. This project eventually lead the Philadelphia Court of Common Pleas to purchase the system. The experiment led also to the publication of the first *User's Guide to Computer-Aided Transcription* (Greenwood 1977). What followed, from 1975 to 1980, was an explosion of CAT system experimentation across the nation. At the time the deciding factor in the evolution of CAT systems was the invention of and introduction of smaller computers—minicomputers and microcomputers. The commercial feasibility of CAT increased as system costs dropped from above $100,000 to below $100,000. Then, as competing firms entered the market, further cost reductions drove down hardware and software costs, so that an individual reporter or very small group could consider the investment. This time the technology was suitable to the reporter profession: it was oriented to the individual person and tailored to specific needs.

From 1975 through 1981 was a period of the first wider experimentation with the initial CAT systems on larger computers. While we have already noted that the Philadelphia system was the leader with much public notoriety, it was soon joined by many other cities—Baton Rouge, Cincinnati, Dallas, Tucson, and Detroit. These early locations were followed by San Antonio, Sacramento, Atlanta, and Phoenix. By the first half of 1980 even more cities joined—Houston, Baltimore, Salt Lake City, Charleston, West Virginia, Tulsa, Honolulu, Reading, and Pittsburgh. This wave of experimentation was just the public side of adopting innovation based on information readily available from studies during the period (Delaplain 1981). As is common with highly successful innovations, the CAT system adoption rate during the period of 1980–1986 has been rapid, climbing about half way up the letter "S" on an S-curve of adoption over the period (Rogers 1983). Due to poor suitability of the early technology for widespread adoption by the reporter profession, from the early 1970s experiments with Avram and Nelson until the end of that decade, acceptance was slow in coming. A current conservative figure is 3,000 CAT systems adoptions, but estimates of three to four times this figure have been suggested.

On the private side, commercial firms scrambled to join and lead the field. Baron*Data*, a firm with early roots, introduced a commercially-viable system in 1976. More recently, strong firms, including Xscribe and the older firm Stenograph Company, have entered the field of CAT technology. It will not be very long before transcription by computers will become *the* dominant modality of reporting transcription work. Let us review these decades of development in the reporter profession from a wider perspective.

The reporting evolution has taken about a century to move from input of oral language to written symbols of shorthand by pen. This was followed by the stenotype machine, which enables reporters to reach the highest input rate of 280 words per minute with high accuracy. On the output side, transcribing slogged along at penmanship rates for all of history until typewriters came along over 100 years ago. Since a typist using a typewriter produces 80 words per minute with high accuracy and even less output under a variety of conditions, there is simply no match between computer-aided transcription and any other form of transcription. Computers produce print at the rate of 30 to 180 characters per second; larger computers using line input printers can print 600 to 2000 lines per minute (Frost and Dunlap 1983, 36). This CAT revolution has opened the reporting profession to the entire world of computer technology, automated litigation support, and real-time translation of closed captioning for the deaf and hearing impaired who number more than 15 million persons in the United States. The willingness of reporters to respond to this modern technology has been a very significant event in the history of reporting.

Furthermore, if one couples the rapid adoption of new CAT technology with rapid growth in the legal profession in the last 20 years (more than 650,000 members), it is clear that demand for reporters is at an all-time high (Curran 1986; Halliday 1986). Couple these factors of growth and demand with other major changes in criminal constitutional law and the last 20 years appear as a period of great discontinuity in reporting. A new era has emerged and a new order in reporting is developing. The Gideon v. Wainwright decision of 1963 by the United States Supreme Court, established a national constitutional right to counsel in all felony cases. This was later expanded to include other criminal, juvenile, and correctional proceedings where liberty may be taken by the state. Transcripts for criminal appeals rose rapidly, and the demand for professional services climbed.

Finally, civil litigation which to handles auto accident cases had to grow as the number of private automobiles rose to the multimillion figure it is today. That transportation system produces vast numbers of deaths and injuries every day on a predictable basis as the system expands. All of this increases demand for reporting services for some of the cases requiring litigation. The ultimate conclusion is that the last 25 years, from 1960 to 1985, are unprecedented in the 85-year history of the growth and development of the reporter profession in the United States. The key elements in the formula for growth included notice pleading systems, growth in the legal profession, CAT technology input, rise in litigiousness, expansion of criminal and civil due process, and basic population and commercial growth.

Other Technological Developments

Audio recording and video technology were available after World War II on a wider scale, but for 40 years they had never taken hold of the bench, the bar, or the reporter profession. The way CAT systems have been welcomed by reporters is a great contrast. But audio and video are tried fitfully and sporadically. The abandonments of systems, even statewide systems, is noteworthy, but in spite of this dour record of innovation, there has been a small niche in the ecology of reporting for this technology (Schleich 1985; National Center for State Courts 1986). This technology is used as a backup system for reporters. It is also used in courts where virtually no transcript is needed. Video technology is used by busy professionals for some classes of depositions. Even here, since 1983 the NSRA has certification programs to conform video skills to professional reporter norms. Even with all of this adoption on a minor scale, the truth is that audio and video technology offers old-fashioned, labor intensive, error-prone transcription systems that slog along at 80 words a minute in the face of fierce competition from CAT systems' rapid transcription. However, official court reporters in federal courts face administrative selling of audio systems to federal judges in spite of low levels of judicial and reporter interest (Murphy 1986). The adoption rate of audio technology in the federal courts is further evidence of a technology failing to be adopted because of its unsuitability for most professional court and legal environments.

International Perspectives

Intersteno

Reporters from the United States meet with their counterparts in an organization called Intersteno—The International Federation of Stenography and Typewriting. Intersteno meets every two years with about 25 countries represented. In 1987 it meets in Florence, Italy, to celebrate 100 years of association activity. One important distinction between the United States and other nations is that reporters in the United States serve the courts to a much greater extent than do reporters in other nations, who more often serve legislative bodies. Intersteno focuses upon many issues central to reporters everywhere, such as how to develop an accurate and reliable record in the writing of a proceeding. This affects every nation and the United Nations. Technology issues related to audio recording are global in nature for Intersteno. The comparative linguistic aspects of stenographic theory are examined across languages. The National Shorthand Reporters Association in the United States relates to Intersteno in a variety of ways (Foster 1981).

Selected Survey of Nations

A survey of 60 nations and their reporting practices was begun about a year ago, and finishing this survey is expected to take more time. High levels of variability in practice are the norm in the materials surveyed thus far. The nature of the official languages, the nature of the legal systems, the nature of the governments, the customs, and the traditions of a nation are some of the factors that produce variation. Whether there are schools of systems is not established from the survey, but it is hypothesized that common-law countries, civil-law countries, and socialist countries may fall into similar patterns. The clearest finding, to date, is that the precision of a court record in the state and federal courts in the United States (where word-for-word accuracy is the standard of practice) is the ideal to be achieved to the extent humanly possible. This contrasts sharply with the approximate and generalized court records and the summaries of court testimony provided in other systems in other nations that require records of what is said at prescribed legal events. The implications of this preliminary finding are not well understood at this time. Further research is needed to develop a better understanding of the practices and the underlying theories of reporting.

2

Organizational Theory for Managing Reporters

Management is first thought to be a practical activity. This entire chapter is, thus, a contradiction to many readers, because organizational theory is stressed so much, rather than emphasis being placed on the practical activity of management. Therefore, a justification is appropriate to answer those readers who wonder: why theory? Why build the link between a body of knowledge (organizational theory) and the reporter profession? What are key organizational characteristics of organizations of reporters? Can organizational theory be practical and helpful to a managing reporter? How does theory help us to function on a daily basis when managing and further help us in the long run of career development in management? These and other related questions will be examined in this chapter.

ORGANIZATIONAL THEORY DEFINED

The words "organizational theory" mean four basic things:

1. Getting a broad and more general, abstract knowledge and perspective: (a) of yourself as a manager, (b) of the organization in which you work, (c) of the class of comparable organizations into which yours fits and why it fits, and (d) of the environment within which you work and in which your organization exists. Lifting you from the limited time horizon and geographical limits of your current management position to gain a broader view of management is what is meant by "organizational theory."

2. Gaining a new and expanded vocabulary of key management terms that will help you to comprehend and use organizational theory. Some of the terms are structure, process, and environment.

3. Being able to understand how the chorus of voices and droves of writers

who write and speak about management can be understood, classified, and typed for future reference. How do the popularizers of management, such as the "one-minute manager" types, help and hurt you?

4. Being better equipped to handle the future in a managerial position in a private reporting organization or in an organization such as a court.

ORGANIZATIONAL THEORY MAP

While the body of knowledge is loosely connected, it is called organizational theory. The world has seen hundreds of definitions like that described because any person who thinks, writes, and speaks about management and organizational theory inevitably develops his or her own theory map of the organizational world and modifies the map as new insights are gained over the years.

The organizational theory map that makes sense to me is both rigid and changing. The rigid part of organizational theory is composed of four principal parts—bureaucracy, human relations, systems theory, and contingency theory. The fluid part of the map is composed of changing interest and emphasis among the four rigid parts and the emergence of new parts or combinations of new theories. Turning first to the rigid part, let us develop sketches of the ideas of bureaucracy, human relations, systems theory, and contingency theory.

Bureaucracy

Everyone knows that the FBI is the Federal Bureau of Investigation. It is also a large bureaucracy. There is nothing similar to the FBI in the entire world of reporting. In fact, the total number of FBI personnel is about twice that of people devoted to reporting. One part of the federal government dwarfs the entire profession of reporting. The word "bureau" gives us "bureaucracy," which is a way of viewing, theorizing, and managing both large and small organizations. The idea of a bureaucracy developed as a reaction to personal fiefdoms in governments; bureaucracy today is less personal—even impersonal. You earn your way by merit (not by blood ties, friendships, or other ways such as bribes). In governments, the idea of civil service applies to reinforce a merit approach to promotion and hiring. In a bureaucracy, jobs are defined in writing and linked to one another, and a rational ordering of positions is created—a hierarchy with ranks and status. If you think this is beginning to sound like the army, navy, and other military organizations, you are right. These organizations use the idea of a bureaucracy, too. Specialization of jobs is a hallmark of a bureaucracy.

In a bureaucracy the stress is on organizational continuity. A person is a completely replaceable part of a large organization. The organization that is managed as a bureaucracy goes on even though people in positions come and go. Thus, in the American society, large corporations, large governmental units, and comparable military and religious organizations use the organizational theory of bureaucracy to define and operate themselves every day. In using this theory, some bureaucracies are so large they typically ignore the world around them. The world around them can be divided into two parts: specific environment of the organization and a general environment affecting all organizations. While a large bureaucracy must interact with its specific environment, it could ignore general social and cultural environmental imperatives for a long time. The usual weakness of a bureaucracy is its ingrown tendencies—it gets "blind-sided," and is usually struck down from a direction it was not paying any attention to. Too much bureaucracy can be unhealthy for the organization and can lead to grave insensitivities to clients, customers, and markets.

Reporter organizations are so small in size that there is little use among reporters for the idea of a bureaucracy. But the idea of bureaucracy is so pervasive in our culture that its workings permeate our entire society, and reporters must be able to identify the bureaucratic tendencies influencing them. Large court systems—such as Chicago, Los Angeles, and New York—probably will need bureaucratic ideas for survival. Reporters working in those settings will need to become conversant with bureaucracy in much greater detail than portrayed here. For example, the "bureautic," like neurotic, tendencies of organizational members to write "memos to the file" in order to cover their behinds (CYA), is an example of common behavior.

Human Relations

Since bureaucracies are noted for their insensitive approaches to people and their insistence upon a rational ordering of organizational life, a new way of thinking has been developed: the human relations theory. This approach focuses its attention on people at work. The human relations scholars came from social sciences—sociology, psychology, and others—and asked questions bureaucrats forgot to ask. How do people really get along with one another at work? What do people really think of bosses and coworkers? Who relates to whom at work and why? Why is there such a thing as a rumor mill? What makes people want to work? Why do people quit so often in organization A and not in organization B? These questions either could not be answered by bureaucratic theory, or its advocates did not care to ask and answer such questions. Bureaucracies have blinders—too limited an outlook. As a consequence, those with psychological backgrounds began to probe the behavior and attitudes of people at work. Today, after decades of development, one can safely say that major research efforts have uncovered a very complex and incomplete understanding of human motivation at work. Dozens of schools of thought have emerged. Money, power, prestige, and many other intangible things influence behavior at work. Here the central focus is on people at work as compared with bureaucratic theory where people fit into job descriptions and are interchangeable parts of a large whole.

Systems Theory

As a consequence of a confluence of ideas, the organizational theories that are founded on systems theory and logic are more recent in origin than either bureaucratic or human relations theories. Central to systems theory is cybernetic feedback loops of information similar to the thermostat control on your house furnace. Joined with this is the computer with its complex hardware and software. Systems management and its advocates pose a very rational ordering of organizational life. Examples of systems theory are management of waiting lines, or achievement of critical paths in construction of buildings by coordinating materials, people and money into the reality of concrete, steel, wood, and glass. Precision in construction of $50 million airliners is a must for systems management. According to systems theory, technology drives the organizational structure and organizational processes and determines the nature of human relations at work—how people relate and interact. Systems management is very compelling and tends toward authoritarianism in the same way that bureaucracy drives bureaucrats.

An advancement of systems theory that accommodates people in organizations inside offices instead of factories or production lines uses sociotechnical design to distinguish routine from nonroutine office work and distinguishes management strategies directed toward both sides of the office (Pava 1983). In Chapter 6 of this book, we will be using the concepts developed by Pava to determine how management and technology can meet effectively with CAT technology inside reporter offices.

Given the tendency of systems management, the human being is once again considered an interchangeable part of the person-machine relationship. In this regard, systems management parallels bureaucracy in its view of people at work. The shortcomings are explored further in the personnel material in Chapter 3.

Contingency Theory

Depending upon the environment, the market, or other circumstances—the contingency factors or uncertainties to be faced by managers—one manages and organizes using contingency theory based upon the real environmental and organizational factors at work when management decisions are required moment by moment. The contingency approach to management is very sensitive to the environment. Compared with both bureaucracy and systems theory, there is a vast difference in outlook toward the world beyond the organization. Contingency approaches to management do not have "pat" answers for managers as compared with bureaucracy, human relations and systems theories. "It all depends" is a critical outlook on the world for contingency managers who tend to want to keep their options open for as long as possible.

These four brief sketches are based upon many books, articles, research studies and the firsthand knowledge of organizations that I have personally observed, studied, and managed. Some of the literature is cited elsewhere and will not be repeated here (Saari 1982). For those who wonder how much is written in English about management, just visit a large university that offers a master's degree in either business or public administration. Review the card catalogues and the book shelves to satisfy your curiosity. Read the dozens of monthly journals on the subject. These will stimulate your curiosity, which can then be whetted and directed further by management courses at a local community college or university. Since each sketch could be expanded to book-length form, it is important not to be misled by the brevity of each description of the rigid part of the organizational map. Nor is it necessary for readers who are not familiar with the literature to become intimidated by it. Just becoming aware of the existence of management literature is enough for now. Later chapters will draw upon a theoretical insight; this chapter will have already introduced a reference framework.

THE LINKAGE RATIONALE

At the outset a central question was raised: Why build a link between a body of knowledge (organizational theory) and the activities of the reporter profession? The answer is rather simple. Going back to Chapter 1 of this book, the definition of a profession according to Alfred North Whitehead requires that professional activities be subject to theoretical analysis, and the definition presumes that theoretical conclusions will help to modify professional behavior, making it more effective in a professional sense. This interactive relationship between theory and practice is illustrated by the discovery of germ theory—a theory in medicine that proposed that microorganisms cause infectious, contagious diseases and other conditions. For example, this discovery led to the pasteurization of milk to kill organisms. After about a hundred years of widespread, worldwide recognition of germ theory, we take it for granted that in order to gain better health, we must attack germs, using a myriad of sophisticated and unsophisticated strategies. Washing our hands before eating and the presurgical scrubbing by surgeons tells us how real the theory of germs is. Theory led to modifications of surgical practice in sanitation. Simple blood-letting without a concern for germ theory became unthinkable in the practice of medicine. What are the parallels for linking theory and practice in reporting?

In reporting, most management theories are imported from management experiences in other organizations. However, it can be demonstrated that theory is useful because reporter organizations use human relations theory. They want to encourage high productivity among reporters. Bonuses, modern technology, pleasant working conditions, clear operations manuals, health insurance and other fringe benefit plans all indicate a real concern for the morale of reporters that directly affects organizational productivity, say, in transcript preparation. The human relations theories assert that a variety of factors motivate workers and that employers want to manage by using motivating factors with a concern for productivity. This establishes the link of one theory or set of theories to management of reporter organizations.

At this time, systems theory is being elevated considerably in the eyes of the reporter profession because of the advent of computer—and CAT—technology. Systems management is also sold. That is, companies that manufacture and sell CAT systems *also* presume to tell reporters how to manage the equipment and thereby manage the people who directly use the equipment. Systems theories of management are impinging on the reporter profession with great force. We shall see that sociotechnical systems applied to office work have become relevant to reporters as well when the work of Pava is explored in Chapter 6.

Structuring an impersonal work force through job descriptions of reporters puts bureaucratic theory to work for reporting. Explicitly managing by using strategies directed to stabilizing uncertainties in the organization's environment is using contingency theory wisely. Assuring a continuous flow of work by marketing is a clear strategic choice to level out demand and keep business coming, rather than depending upon chance and market uncertainties.

The four rigid parts of organizational theory do play a significant role in shaping the way reporters relate to one another inside firms and governments. Bureaucracy, human relations, systems theory, and contingency theory can be used in a wide variety of ways by managers to analyze their effectiveness as managers.

ORGANIZATIONAL CHARACTERISTICS

What are the key organizational characteristics of reporter organizations? Perhaps most vivid are the public-private distinctions in reporting that become modified as we will see in Chapter 4 on finance and in Chapter 5 on marketing. If data from the National Shorthand Reporters Association on registered and participating membership is indicative, we can see a total of about 16,000 professional members. It is clear that about three-quarters of the members are in private practice while one-quarter are in public positions. Three out of four reporters work in a private setting; every one of four reporters works in a public setting. Public reporter offices are as large as

300 reporters, while private reporter offices probably do not exceed 50 members. Public reporters are affected by the public budget processes and public personnel systems. Private reporters are free of these public constraints and many are independent contractors answerable only to the clients and to themselves. However, many reporters in the private sector are employees of reporting firms whose employers must withhold income and social security taxes, pay unemployment benefits, pay worker compensation insurance coverage, respond to Fair Labor Standards Act for overtime for employees, and finally, as we have seen in New York City in the introduction to this book, be subject to union rules, union contracts, and collective bargains with employees. These are significant differences among various types of reporters.

In general, the size of reporter organizations is small even though we have suggested already that there are very large public organizations of reporters in the largest metropolitan courts of the nation like Chicago and Los Angeles. These are the exception. With small size comes increased face-to-face contact and managerial responses relevant in such a setting.

Not much is known quantitatively on a national basis about the reporter's race, sex, age, and education except for observations and opinion from knowledgeable experts. The reporter profession is believed to be dominantly white and female with the largest numbers in the 20 to 40 age range. The education of the largest number includes the completion of high school and reporter school. Reporter schools are filled with younger women seeking a career. Those who have been in the field many years say that there were many more men reporters in the past. This suggests a trend toward feminization of the reporter profession in the long run. Yet, these stereotypes based on opinion are inadequate to explain who survives in the reporter profession for 5 years, 10 years, or 20 years. Who cycles in, who stays, who leaves? We simply do not know. Managers of reporters represent another human profile that is older and more experienced, with a more balanced male/female ratio. There are other unknowns—such as regional and state variations, or urban and rural differences—that could shape our understanding of the reporter profession. Having experienced several national meetings of reporters, I have seen great diversity in sex, age, race, education, and experience in the field.

Specialization within the reporting field is significant. Pen writers, stenotype writers, CAT writers, video specialists, audio specialists, scopists, typists, editors, accountants, note readers, supervisors, and managers are evident. Private reporting firms have enthusiastically embraced CAT technology in the last five years. Much specialization is in the private sector of the profession. Also, the marketing of reporter services is a locally directed effort in the community, but reporters are now joining national groups to market services on a national basis. This follows the pattern used by law firms that have a national group of offices.

THE LEGAL ENVIRONMENT

One dominant, specific environmental factor that affects almost all reporters is the legal community. This part of the reporter's environment includes practicing lawyers, trial judges, prosecutors, defenders, courthouse staffs, law firm staffs, and many others associated with the law. This is a highly literate milieu of professionals and supporting personnel of whom the reporter group is one among many. The law firm is a logical organizational form; the solo practitioner is another. This suggests that reporter firms are organized, structured, and made relevant to the world around them in ways similar to those of other organizations in their environment.

PROFESSIONALLY DOMINATED ORGANIZATIONS

Reporters who organize into private organizations have a ready-made, well-established organizational model to follow—the private law firm in corporate or partnership form. The private reporter firms range from highly structured employer-employee relationships to unstructured conglomerates of independent contractors who associate in a minimal way. In either distinctive form, reporter firms are characterized in organizational theory to be professionally dominated organizations. This suggests that reporters are in charge of their own organizations and that professional standards come first in deciding all critical issues.

Think of other professionally dominated organizations. They include court systems with judges, universities and colleges with professors, research and development firms with scientists, and firms of lawyers, architects, and physicians. All of these illustrate the wide range of professionally dominated organizations. Private reporter firms with professional reporters in charge of the firm represent another example of such an organization. There are dual lines of authority—the professionals in one group and the support staffs in another (Mintzberg 1979). These organizations are flat in structure with few layers of hierarchy as compared with the tall pyramids of big bureaucracies. There is little review of management decisions, and there are few layers of control, since professionals are supposed to discipline and control themselves while practicing. These are the identifying structural characteristics of professionally dominated organizations. Direct client service is another hallmark—where professionals serve and interact directly with students, research laboratories, clients, or patients. No managerial intermediary is consulted when providing legal, medical, or architectural advice directly to others. Reporters do work directly in trials, hearings, conventions, and depositions with *no* management intermediary to supervise their professional work.

The central motif of professionally dominated organizations is that of offering service, a calling that can be expressed only through direct exercise of judgment by the professional. No administration or managerial person can exercise the power and judgment of a professional. For example:

- Professors in universities authorize grades for students.
- Physicians prescribe medicine and medical advice.
- Lawyers advise clients.
- Surgeons cut human flesh.
- Scientists personally conduct experiments.
- Pharmacists dispense medicine.
- Judges personally sign judgment orders determining rights with finality.

In a parallel way, as a professional, the reporter certifies the transcript of a proceeding, a trial, or deposition. Not just any reporter can certify and managers cannot certify. The one who renders the professional reporting service signs the certification. This is similar to judges, who cannot "unsign" another judge's order or sign for something they did not hear. The stamp of individuality marks a scientific study, a memorandum of legal opinion, and a grade for a student. The notes and transcripts of reporters have this same stamp of individuality, the same personal quality, the same professional trait.

Why is the professional service so important? The reason is simple: professional service is the principal reason for the existence of the private reporter firm. For reporters employed by court systems, the bureaucratic nature of many of those organizations affects the perspective that reporters are independent professionals, but that also happens to judges and lawyers who work for the government. There are professionally dominated organizations—some hospitals, for example—where the professionals have lost control to owners and managers. This has happened to some institutions of higher education where administrators and trustees have displaced the professional domination and professional standards of professors. But if physicians refused to treat patients in a hospital, or if professors refused to teach in a university, the rationale for the organization would soon come to an abrupt halt. The same is true of reporters. Reporters who practice in their own private firms realize the service they provide directly to law firms and individual lawyers. And reporters who work in public organizations such as courts recognize the central nature of their work. But reporters have met administrators in the federal courts, for example, who question both the professional nature of reporter work and other attributes of professionalism. When these doubts arise, administrative standards clash with professional standards and disagreements result. The administrators of federal courts are presently in the middle of this type of conflict with the reporter profession. It has happened on a state level as well. But some perspective is necessary. Engineers face challenges to their professional work from managers. Physicians employed by hospitals find organizational standards of practice clashing with their professionally-established standards. Conflicts of this nature are common phenomena in professionally-dominated organizations.

HUMAN SERVICE PROFESSIONAL MODEL

In Chapter 1, the human service model of reporting was developed. This model is directly relevant to the discussion of professional standards in organizations. It should be clear that the human service model of reporting supports the professional nature of the work of reporters. This model proposes that the transformation of language from oral to written form is a filtering process done by a specific human being in a specific setting. For example, reporters do their professional reporting in courtrooms, their conference rooms, lawyer's conference rooms, and in a wide range of other places such as conventions and administrative hearings. The service is provided under professional standards that are carried with the reporter wherever reporting needs to be done. This is no different from legal professionals who provide service in a wide variety of settings. This suggests that the norms of good professional practice are transportable—they are practiced outside of the organization and are not dependent on the organization or management for enforcement.

Keep in mind that organizational theory offers one an opportunity to see how reporter organizations are confronted with difficulties that are similar to the difficulties of other professionally-dominated organizations. The point is this: The organization associated with a practicing reporter should not discount or disparage professional reporting standards and norms by trying to displace them with norms the organization thinks serves the organization the best. In this struggle, professional norms, standards, and judgments must prevail over the organization's views, otherwise the organization rather than the individual reporter is attempting to become a profession. Could the organization certify the transcript as an organization? What would that mean? Since no profession is exercised by a fictional entity called an organization but by specific, qualified human beings, it is these human beings who are personally responsible for their actions.

Reporters who become deeply involved with organizations will see the potential for erosion of professional standards as organizations intrude themselves, through their managers, into professional judgments. It does seem to be an unfortunate tendency in today's society, and unless the intrusive nature of management controls is confronted directly by professionals, there will be continual unwarranted intrusion into the professional lives of reporters. Unfortunately, organizational theory related to professionally dominated organizations does not prescribe answers. However, I have interjected some of my views into this analysis. The theory merely makes the nature of the conflict very clear.

When judges and court administrators intervene in reporting by insisting upon total video or total audio recording, they substitute their judgment for the professional judgment of reporters. When this is done, there is a very high risk of failure and long-term rejection that will haunt these judges and court administrators who refuse to acknowledge expertise beyond their organizational power. It is unwise to replace the professional judgments of reporters. It suggests to me a belief that a mechanical model of reporting, which is nonprofessional in nature, could operate validly in a professional manner. This is a contradiction that hardly merits attention. The mechanical model of reporting is rejected by professional reporters and is fought vigorously wherever it arises. The organization that is sold on the mechanical model of reporting, that denies the professionalism of reporters, is doomed to repeat the mistakes that have plagued courts for years. Reporting is a professional activity in which judgment is exercised, and no desire for organizational efficiency or accuracy can drive the professional nature of the work out of existence. Therefore, it is the professional norms that will ultimately dominate in any organization where reporters work professionally. After all, lawyers insist upon legal and judicial norms in their decisions and support management standards that permit them to do professional work. Why should reporters defer to standards of reporting outside of their profession? The general tendency I have observed is a gradual debasement of high-quality professional reporting standards when reporters allow nonreporter standards to intrude into their domain of expertise. Everything in organizational theory calls for sensitive attention to professional relationships in a professionally dominated organization. If managers of reporter organizations (who may themselves be reporters) are aware of these issues outlined, they will be aware of the need to seek intelligent accommodation of organizational norms and standards to professional norms and standards wherever possible. That is the pathway toward high-quality professional reporting.

LEADERSHIP

Another contribution of organization research and theorizing has been in the area of leadership. Everyone who manages should be amazed that, most of the time, people will do what their managers ask them to do. On its face that appears to be management leadership. But what about professional persons who do what needs to be done without leadership from an organizational source? Or what about those who do what is needed in spite of contrary views of organizational leaders? In general, professionals do not require leaders; they lead themselves. It is only when professionals form organizations that leadership begins to be a source of potential difficulty. But leadership need not be a negative factor.

It is comforting to note that, for many decades, research has not uncovered the secrets of leadership. Leonard Sayles suggests: "Most human behavior experts have become wary of trying to correlate personality traits with executive performance and for good reason. The typical personality test used as a selection was never very good, and it was often prejudicial and misleading" (Sayles 1979, 240). But Sayles and others have not given up the search for understanding the phenomenon of leadership in organizations. Most leadership research is done in organizations that have a few professional staff specialists. As a result, the issues are not as clear as those in the reporter organizations where professionals dominate. Earlier in this chapter, the professionally dominated organization was outlined in some detail, including the struggles it has with management.

According to contingency theory, managers who are in leadership roles have direct responsibility to develop contingency responses to reduce uncertainty. This may involve assertion of authority and building commitment and motivation. Managers do this by handling lateral relations inside and outside the organization, trying to gain power in both arenas. They work the hierarchy of the organization. They develop acceptable controls. And they introduce change to respond to organizational needs (Sayles 1979). In a professional organization, team building among experts is another illustration of management leadership. Management should not be viewed as an interference but as a means of supporting professionals in organizations that offer professional service. Shared leadership models seem to be the only tenable models appropriate to reporter organizations.

Dysfunctions of leadership are well known. The unbearable boss makes life miserable for everyone. The bad bosses cannot be trusted, are ruthless and bullheaded, treat employees disrespectfully, often dodge responsibility, or are plainly incompetent but do not admit it (Goleman 1986). The pain that bad leadership inflicts on organizational members can be an unforgettable experience. Reporter organizations are not immune from such problems.

A recent aspect of leadership that is important for reporters is the assessment of feminine leadership styles. Marilyn Loden has developed a thesis that men and women differ in approaches to leadership. According to Loden, women need to nurture the style that suits them—and that style is not mirroring what men do to lead (Loden 1985). With the high proportion of women in reporting and the high probability that women will be holding leadership positions in the field of reporting in the future, the issues of leadership developed by Loden are significant to reporters. Loden finds two models of leadership with differing operating styles, organizational structures, basic objectives, problem-solving styles, and key characteristics (Loden 1985, 26 and 63). In these areas men are more competitive, inclined toward hierarchy, win-oriented, more rational, desirous of control, more analytical, and are strategy makers. Women in leadership tend to be more cooperative, team-oriented, interested in quality output, reasonably cautious less interested in control, more empathetic and are collaboraters and high performers. Why and how this could be so is explained by Loden. For reporters, it is a theoretical aspect to leadership that could well develop into a significantly practical application for managing reporters more effectively.

MANAGING UNCERTAINTY

Leadership is not the only place where contingency theory is important. A managing reporter faces uncertainty on many fronts: Employees become ill, develop attitudes that hinder cooperation, become pregnant, and quit work. The competitive environment for a private free-lance reporting firm can become a nightmare with costs rising out of sight, income dropping because of business lost to competitors, unexpected repair bills, and changes in tax laws. A new legislature can slash government budgets; a new governor with a new agenda can place reporters' hopes for modernization on hold for a long time; and a new chief justice or presiding judge can emphasize some other part of operations giving reporters scarce resources.

Uncertainty is the hallmark of organizational life and is a central factor for managing reporters. One way to treat uncertainty is to ignore it. Another strategy is to pay attention only to those things that interest you. Those who have developed the contingency theory believe that the manager has difficulty comprehending all of the potential external environmental sources of uncertainty and equal difficulty learning about all of the internal sources of uncertainty in the organization. The manager has a fragile understanding of what may come next. If this is a truthful state of affairs, managers have plenty to deal with. When you think of all the potential blockage points in the smooth flow of getting a deposition and delivering a transcript, or reporting a trial and delivering a transcript, you comprehend the manager's need to pay attention to detail and, at the same time, to keep the "big picture" of the organization in mind. This duality is very difficult for most managers who work with the contingency theory on a daily basis.

An added source of frustration for managers is the demand on their time for brief phone calls and personal contacts to the point that their attention span is equated with that of a butterfly as it flits from flower to flower. This disjointed day is the norm for many managers, particularly in smaller organizations where the manager is actively involved in the operations of the business (Mintzberg, 1973). Just trying to survive is a major job for managers in a fast-moving organization. Deadlines increase stress, and energy levels rise and fall as deadlines come and go. This complication of real-world management, with all its pressures and unforeseen contingencies, makes management a difficult, demanding job that few people know enough about before being thrust into the work. Organizational theory can be seen as a rudder which guides one's thoughts about management. Steering an intelligent course through each day of managing is a neccesary goal, and the tools of organizational theory will help to achieve that goal. These tools are sketched in this chapter so that a better understanding of management can be pursued. And the theory lays a foundation for the chapters to follow.

3

Personnel Management for Managing Reporters

People are the most complicated, most expensive, and most unpredictable of all parts of an organization (Miner 1985). The complexity, expense, and uncertainty of human beings in organizations has kept people in the spotlight for managers, organizational theorists, and union organizers. Each of the organizational theories described in the previous chapter offers a view of human nature implicit in the theory. Bureaucratic theory offers a not-too-flattering view of people in which they occupy positions, are to be limited and bounded by authority and power, are to be controlled by the discipline of a higher authority, and are replaceable parts of the organization. One person is just like another—a pair of hands is a pair of hands. You sit in a little box and do what you are told. Initiative is not warmly welcomed. Bureaucracies, in general, belittle human nature by reducing the person to an object to be controlled, by denying individuality, and by encouraging team spirit above all. Bureaucracies take that complicated, expensive, and unpredictable thing called a human being and develop strategies to reduce complexity, to search for the least expensive person, and to control their unpredictability. Where bureaucracy thrives, in the military and large paramilitary organizations, for example, this view of human nature at work is premised on a potentially hostile environment—say in war or in law enforcement work against criminal drug merchants. The bureaucratic view of human nature is, fortunately, just one of many views.

Human relations theories pose organizational strategies for managing people that are much more in tune with the complicated, expensive, and unpredictable nature of human beings at work. Some say the theories are too liberal a view. However, these strategies are suitable in a egalitarian and democratic society such as ours. The dominant chord of human relations theories is human individuality, the understanding of that individuality, and the promotion of individuality in ways that suit the organization. When the aims of individuals and organizations harmonize, the human relations school will say that heaven has been achieved. None of the advocates believes in a naive view of human nature. Since freedom to leave the organization is respected, the human relations school proposes to reduce the turnover rate of employees to a bare minimum, thereby indicating effectiveness of managing people. People stay where they know that they are wanted and needed.

The systems theory views human beings as extensions of machines, as little black boxes on flow diagrams through which there is input and output. Yet the black-boxed person is controlled at both ends of input and output. People in systems are interchangeable, as in a bureaucracy, and the cost, complexity, and unpredictability of people are "engineered around" by wise systems experts. As Curt Suplee states about new computer design: "And the nets' self-programming ability could save us from ourselves." Quoting a source for his article he writes, " 'Most people who use a computer make mistakes, type the wrong keys. Well, we could have a keyboard that simply remembers your corrections and leaves the patterns.' Then when you hit the wrong key, 'it would end up doing what you mean, not what you say' " (Suplee 1986).

The suggestion of machines that save us from our mistake-making selves clearly identifies where superiority lies in the man–machine interface. The machines are superior. As I indicated before in Chapter 1, the mechanical model of reporting is defective because it is based upon this type of systems/machine oriented mentality. Systems and computers are seen as superior to bumbling human beings. Man is a fool who needs a machine to keep him from error.

Finally, the complexity, expense, and unpredictability of human beings is taken in stride by contingency theories. So what if the human dimension of an organization has these characteristics? So what if people create errors? Every other part of organizational life is the same in nature, thus nothing special needs to be done to manage human beings. You take people as they are, and work with them—trying to study their errors, complexity, expense, and unpredictability by developing contingency plans for each source of perturbation in the organization. The contingency theory does not posit any type of human nature. It can work with the human relations theories when helpful or with systems or bureaucratic theories when helpful. In this sense, contingency theory is the most inclusive theory for managing. Perhaps the strongest feature of contingency theory lies in its willingness to accept the world as it is and *not* attempting to remake the human being into any preconceived notion of how people should act at work. Thus, it is the freest form of managing within the social, cultural, and legal norms of organizations. It offers an approach to managing that elevates flexibility, but it is not unprincipled flexibility where managers are free to do anything that pleases them. Contingency management is done within an environment that takes all types of constraints, habits, customs, regulations, laws, and mores into account. This is especially true in the personnel field as we shall see in this chapter.

Besides the theoretical view of human nature, there are three important avenues to examine in personnel management in the reporter field. The first is an analysis of types of reporters and types of employment or other contractual relationships in the field. There are significant differences in the relationships among reporters and in reporters' relationships with governments that deserve thorough attention because they are so basic. For some reporters these relationships are a source of concern. The second major area is supervision of reporters. What are the central concerns? Why is supervision so important? Finally, the selection of reporter employees is a critical art that deserves a significant place when thinking about managerial tasks for managing reporters. Obviously, there are important topics *not* addressed in this chapter—pay and fringe benefit programs, training and continuing education needs, and many other personnel topics. These will have to be covered by a special volume on personnel issues and not by one such as this that is devoted to broad managerial perspectives on reporting.

The reporters of the nation are related to their work in a variety of patterns that are rather complex. The dimensions that will be explored here include the public–private dimension and the independent contractor–employee dimension. Some typologies of reporters will be offered to assist in analyzing personnel management problems. Let us start with the public–private dimension.

PUBLIC-PRIVATE DIMENSIONS

Official Reporters

Reporters who fall within a strictly public category of reporting are called official reporters, since they have been appointed to a public position by an official order signed by a judge or some other official. A pure official reporter position is one where the reporter reports all trials, sentencings, motions, and any other matter where a record is required or desired for a particular judge. This type of reporter usually acts as a secretary to the judge who appointed him or her. This type of official reporter does not report for other judges, does not assist other reporters, and does not report for members of the bar for deposition activity. The main thrust of the work of the pure official reporter is directed exclusively to one judge. Frequently, the reporter serves at the pleasure of the judge and is appointed under a state statute that designates the power of the judge to make such appointments. Thus, this pure official reporter is essentially a "loner"—a person whose professional reporting activity is devoted exclusively to serving another public official.

No one intervenes in this contractual relationship without the consent of the judge and the reporter. Other judges and court administrators have little or no say in this relationship. There is no union making its wishes known. It usually reaches its purest form in rural settings where the one-to-one relationship of trial judge and reporter is the only feasible method of making a record in the location or various locations in which the judge may sit in a multiple courthouse district. The salary of this reporter is usually set in a state statute passed by the legislature establishing a statewide salary for all reporters. The package of fringe benefits varies considerably. The state treasury or the county treasury may be the source of payment of salary and fringe benefits, and we could conceive of a state-county combination of reporter support. Transcription fees are paid in addition to salary in nearly every state (Kotzan 1984). Whether the pure official reporter described here is a state or county employee, or a mixed employee, or is classified as a contractual employee depends upon state law. From this single, pure type of official report secretary there has evolved a wide range of types of official reporters.

A study of court reporting practices in state court systems was conducted by the Conference of State Court Administrators (Kotzan 1984). This study involved a detailed written questionnaire covering a broad range of topics, sent to every state and territory. The return was very high—93% from 49 states and two territories. No response was received from Pennsylvania, American Samoa, Guam, or the Virgin Islands. The wide variety of "official reporter" employment relationships is a significant finding of the study:

- State-employed Reporters—40 of 51 (78%) of the areas surveyed indicated that the state did employ reporters. In 21 states, the respondents said the state is the *sole* employer, but in 19 states, the state is *not* the sole employer.
- Locally-employed Reporters—18 of 51 (35%) of the reporting places said localities (cities or counties) employed reporters. In five places, the county or city is the *sole* employer, but in 13 reporting places, the locality is *not* the sole employer.
- Joint Public/Private Reporters—16 of 51 (31%) of the reporting places stated that reporters are employed jointly by the government and by court reporting firms or associations.
- Self-employed Reporters—20 of 51 (39%) of the reporting places indicated that reporters were self-employed, free-lance workers, and that the government was one of the clients of the reporter.

The information is not clear by itself, but another part of the same study sheds some light on whether reporters work for an individual judge or whether they are pooled. The same 1984 study indicated that 25 of 40 jurisdictions responding to the question use individual assignment systems, but only five jurisdictions reported pooling of reporters. These jurisdictions are Connecticut, District of Columbia, Maine, New York, and Vermont.

Another ten jurisdictions pool and individually assign reporters—Alabama, Delaware, Florida, Hawaii, Illinois, Louisiana, Michigan, Mississippi, New Hampshire, New Jersey, Ohio, Oregon, Tennessee, and Wisconsin. There was a significant amount of pooling of reporters in a wide range of states in 1984. If you couple the three employer sources—state, county/city, and private firms—with self-employment status, and then note the pooling of reporters, it is clear that official reporters viewed from a national perspective are not one homogeneous group. There is no pure official type of reporter in the United States other than the one that we described. It is safe to conclude that the approximately 4,000 reporters who belong to NSRA in the "official" category represent an extremely diverse set of individuals with employment contracts that display this diversity.

In the "official" capacity one could ask who, besides the reporter managing himself or herself, is responsible for management of reporters. There were more than ten answers offered in the 1984 study: trial court judges, administrative law judge, in-court supervisor, clerk of court, supervising reporter, coordinator of transcription services, state coordinator of court reporters, trial court administrators, state personnel officer, state court administrator, trial court clerk, attorneys, and others. This diversity should help to eradicate the view that there is a single managerial type associated with the official reporter (Kotzan 1984). And it seems likely that professional reporter work would also face this diversity of management by outsiders in the public arena. Dual supervision of judges and court administrator is likely in many facets of professional reporting.

One other significant hallmark of a reporter's status of employment is the widespread use of separate compensation to official reporters who prepare transcripts of official proceedings (Kotzan 1984). Of the 50 reporting jurisdictions who answered this question, 48 jurisdictions noted that court reporters receive transcript fees in addition to salary. Only Delaware and Puerto Rico combine salary and transcript fees. This means that across the entire nation reporters in an "official" capacity who are required to prepare transcripts of civil and criminal cases must do so, but they are compensated separately for the transcript on a fee arrangement. The fee structures, usually a page rate, are established in state laws and court rules. Transcripts for indigent are paid by governments. The income of official reporters, then, varies depending upon the transcription load and type facing each reporter. And the load and type vary over time.

One could ask, why is there such complexity of compensation for official reporters? The probable answer is that reporters are personally responsible for certifying the transcripts that are prepared from their notes. State laws usually mandate this practice. The reporters' notes are their property and their professional product in the way that a lawyer's notes are his professional product. In addition, stenographic written or stenotyped notes are best read by the writer of those notes. Only if a reporter dies, gets sick, or is absent has another reporter been officially designated to read the absent reporter's notes and certify the transcript. While CAT technology allows reporters' dictionaries to be placed on disks, these disks are each reporter's personal property. Thus, the way a reporter's notes may be certified, once transcribed, and the way the reporters are typically paid for transcriptions on a page-rate basis influences the nature of the reporter's government employment relationship when it comes to reporting in a public courtroom. Salary and fee go hand in hand due to the nature of the work.

Private, Free-Lance Reporters

The NSRA membership includes about 10,000 persons who call themselves free-lance reporters. Free-lance describes an independent status; it suggests that one is pursuing a profession without long-term contractual commitments to any one employer or customer. There are free-lance photographers, free-lance writers, and free-lance reporters. The words "free lance" are often meant to be the equivalent of self-employed, a term used to describe reporters in this private category. Free-lance status and independent contractor status are closely associated. There are also private associations of reporters, all of whom practice together, say in one office, but who maintain their separate identity. Then there are reporters who work together in a firm, but submerge their separate identities to an organizational image and legal entity—either a corporation, a partnership, or a sole proprietorship that employs some of the reporters. The latter form is usually a partnership with partners and employees, or a corporation with shareholders, officers, and employees. Finally, there are firms of reporters who hire unionized federation reporters, as in New York City, where the relationship has grown into one between a principal reporter and a union federation reporter, all private and, for the most part, free-lance in nature.

There are other ways reporters relate to one another, and the best that can be said is that this side of private reporting is filled with great employment diversity. Just as "official reporter" cloaks a varied real world, so "free-lance reporter" cloaks a wide range of employment relationships. For example, a private reporting firm could easily develop a contract with a public court system to provide reporting services when needed. One client of a private reporter firm could be a government or different governments. Reporters can agree among themselves to any sort of relationship and can bargain over whatever they wish, so long as it is not illegal and does not violate public policy. Reporters in the private arena can work with whomever they choose, may restrict or expand their services, may use any type of reporting technology or system, and have the freedom to do contractually whatever suits them. This freedom of a free-lance reporter is an attractive feature of the reporter profession. Offering personal service in this manner is one of the fastest growing parts of the American economy. And the free-lance reporter lies at the very heart of the legal community by performing the vital function of taking depositions, and in reporting any meeting a client wishes to have reported, whether it involves the law or not. For example, many reporters are reporting conventions and conferences, thereby making written records of the official meetings of various groups. This example suggests that free-lance reporters are confronted with a wide range of clients, a wide range of reporting locations, and a wide variety of expectations about their performance. Closed-captioning printing on the television screen is prepared for deaf viewers by reporters. There seems to be an expansion of private reporter services.

A strictly private reporter could be reporting alone, out of his or her own office, with his or her own staff of receptionist, typist, notereader or CAT scopist, and other office personnel, with a wide variety of clients in law firms and elsewhere, and with a schedule to suit the aims of the private reporter. The reporter could work as hard as the demand for services in the community would permit. One's reputation as a reporter would be established in a local community, but private reporters could be referred reporting business from other reporters elsewhere in the community, state, or nation. Some private reporters must take their reporting activity to Europe or the Far East when clients demand their services overseas. This sketch describes the purest solo reporter practitioner which parallels the work of the solo lawyer with his staff and clients.

PROFIT MOTIVE

Perry Moore states: "The most significant difference between public and private personnel management results from lack of the profit motive in public organizations" (Moore 1985,3). He reasons that the "bottom line" of profit motive requires managers of private organizations to be very cautious about overstaffing on one hand and encouraging productive employees through greater rewards on the other. The control of labor costs is the central feature of private reporting, whereas public organizations have less pressure on them based upon the following rationale. According to Moore, in the public organization:

1. Managers may tend to attract and select public employees based on political loyalty, interest group representation, affirmative action or veterans preference while competence may take a back seat to those factors.

2. The quality, quantity, and timeliness of public service is more important than the cost of service.

3. Seniority and step salary increases in an automatic manner eliminate arguments about merit in work.
4. Frustration, wasted time, and risk result when attacking substandard performance or when dismissing public employees who usually have strong due process and union rights.
5. Growth in public salaries is difficult to halt because entire job classes and their descriptions may need to be redrafted to combat what is called grade inflation.

These five factors make management of official reporters even more difficult in an already complex situation where professional work is being coordinated and supervised to the greatest possible extent. The public reporter who must manage other public reporters is constrained by this same logic. Thus, controlling labor costs has been affected by environmental factors such as declines in tax revenues during recessions, citizens voting "no" on tax increases at the local level, and citizens taking political action to reduce taxes. These political constraints have thrown public managers into budget reduction modes of operation or "cut-back management." In these environmental conditions, the managing reporter is faced with external forces that impinge directly on what can be done to control labor costs in reporting. So even if reporters want higher salaries and greater fees from transcript work in the public sector, they are faced with very powerful political constraints in federal, state, and local governments. Indirectly, the political constraints become similar to the profit motive for private reporters. Both constraints keep managers on their toes and if a reporter firm is working in both the public and private sectors of reporting at the same time, these dual political and profit-motive constraints operate beside one another to act as a check on excessive labor costs.

INDEPENDENT CONTRACTOR/EMPLOYEE CONTINUUM

One of the more troublesome and confusing areas of personnel management involves employment relationships that are characterized or mis-characterized depending upon who is involved. The question is really a series of questions about how two reporters relate to one another and the consequences of the relationship. Sometimes two people may intend one thing, but others see something else in the relationship. Before reporter personnel problems are mentioned, there is a good example to keep in mind that illustrates what is meant by characterizing or mis-characterizing a relationship.

The example involves an adult man and woman who live together, call themselves husband and wife, yet have never been civilly or religiously married. This couple does not have a description other than "unrelated households" as accorded by the United States Bureau of Census. These people are "sinners" in the eyes of some religious folks. But if they carry on the relationship long enough, their personal property and real estate titles are truly impacted when the law places a common law marriage upon the relationship, so that in the event of separation or death, the separation of property and passing of half the title at death can be legally installed in the name of the survivor. Who is concerned about the relationship and why can be significant, and the time of concern is important.

Who could be concerned about the relationship of one reporter to another? The federal, state, and local taxing authorities for income taxes, withholding taxes or estimates, for social security payments, for insurance to pay for worker's compensation benefits during injury at work; courts for common law liability of a master for torts of a servant at work; union relationships and collective bargaining under the federal or state labor laws; and enforcers of the Fair Labor Standards Act for payment of overtime to employees who work more than forty hours a week. In general, if two reporters relate as completely independent contractors who share no space, employees, or costs, and they develop a simple letter of understanding about how they will work together on a single case at one time in their lives, they have a fairly clear independent contractor relationship for a limited time and a limited purpose. Payments between them are income to one and expenses to the other for work under the contract.

Now suppose the two reporters start to relate to one another on a continuous basis over time. Income, expenses, and space could be shared, or one could start to draw a salary while the other does not. Does one become an employee and the other an employer, or do they remain two independent contractors pooling resources? Are they partners? Is it a sole proprietorship with one employee—the reporter who draws the salary? During the course of a relationship, the free-lance reporter who thought he or she was an independent contractor could find that he or she became an employer or employee. Once *employee status* is achieved or found to be so by one of many outside interests, then a large avalanche of consequences follows. The employer finds federal law insisting upon an employer identification tax number, and salary payments must be listed and taxes withheld for federal and often state government. These different governments expect the employers to pay the withheld amounts promptly and periodically during the year. Social security payments withheld from employees, and the employer's contributions to social security must be paid frequently. Unemployment compensation payments by an employer to a state must also be paid. Workers who are employees are, by law, required to be covered by insurance for injuries on the job. The Fair Labor Standards Act requires employers to pay time and half when an employee works over forty hours a week. Private insurance programs for health, liability, and life insurance cover employees but not independent contractors. In addition, a person who remains an independent contractor—a *nonemployee*—is *not* subject to income tax withholding, social security, unemployment compensation, overtime pay, or worker's compensation. And many reporters are independent contractors. They are not employees. For example, it is usually true that no space, no telephone, no office furniture, no secretarial services, and nothing else associated with coming to work in someone else's office is provided in the genuine independent contractor relationship. They do not share accounting services, they do not share income and expenses, they file separate tax returns, and they bill one another in writing for service and expect payment by check that is reported as independent contractor income and expense. It seems so simple and so rewarding to attain and sustain an independent contractor status.

First, since you are in business as a reporter and operating as an independent contractor, all of your expenses to produce reporter income are deductible for federal and usually state income tax purposes. The office rental, maintenance, telephone, heat, light, air conditioning, all office amenities and all equipment—CAT, copiers, laser printers, complex phone systems, and employee expenses—are deductible as regular business expenses. So far no tax act dissolves this advantage, and it may never be changed as an advantage for independent contractors. With tax advantages such as these, there are liability advantages as well: two independent contractors are not generally liable to each other's clients. So why is there a problem?

The problem arises because two or more independent reporters relate to one another in some hybrid or mixed relationship that looks like an employee relationship but is not intended to be one. One example would be where a reporter firm would develop a series of permanent relationships by written contract with a number of independent contract reporters who work at home or in other offices. No office is provided, but reporting work is referred through the network, common advertising expense may be shared, and perhaps other expenses may be pooled. Everyone acts independently, but there are regular flows of communication about jobs to do, jobs done, clients billed, fees shared, periodic common meetings, and other indicia of an organization, even though there are no true employees except a handful in a central office. This cottage industry approach in networking that computers may enhance through independent, stand-alone personal computers raises an interesting question for governmental officials charged with collecting taxes, social security, unemployment benefits, and overtime payments, and others concerned with health, life, accident, liability and other insurance concerns. The hybrid, or mixed, set of relationships among reporters carries with it certain risks of ambiguity in the eyes of governments and businesses. The manager has a clear choice: is the risk worth the trouble because other advantages outweigh a clear organizational situation in the eyes of the law or other businesses?

SUPERVISION AND COORDINATION

The central problem of personnel management on a day-by-day, hour-by-hour, and minute-by-minute basis is supervision. Those who supervise and those who are supervised tangle with one another in the most predictable and unpredictable manners. They are thrown together and must work side by side for long periods of time. The pressure cooker position of supervisor is looked down on from above, and is looked down on from below. What this suggests is that the bosses of supervisors do not like them, and the employees who must be supervised do not like them. Certainly this is an exaggerated view. Although much attention has been paid to supervision in the field of personnel management, there is no formula to hand to a manager and say, "go forth and supervise well, you have the golden key." Sometimes the Ten Commandments and the Golden Rule seem to be the only supervision rules that make sense. But "doing unto others what you would have them do to you" often deteriorates into "do unto others as they do to you." With a slight change, the Golden Rule becomes a rule of revenge. For all of the reasons specified above, and more that will be invented by fighting people in the future, supervision is an art that taxes the most patient manager. How can a reporter, who has to manage other reporters and support staff, provide the most effective management and supervision?

It would help if we gave some content to the words "effective management and supervision." The first lesson is one of size. Supervision difficulties increase significantly with the size of the organization. On the public side, there is minimal supervision needed when one judge and one reporter relate in a trial court. As the number of judges in a trial court increases to about ten, the one judge–one reporter system works rather smoothly. But sometime after the 10th judge is added to a courthouse and before the 20th judge is added, the relationships become increasingly complex, especially in the urban areas of America. At the very upper end of current complexity are Chicago and Los Angeles both with more than 300 plus public official reporters, many locations, complex management plans, complex financing, difficult coordination of trial attorneys, and demand for reporters in very complex space. Los Angeles court reporters in the Superior Court work with a 65-page personnel manual that covers topics for supervision: recruitment, examination, selection and placement, compensation and payroll procedures, employee performance evaluation, working hours and leave, conduct and responsibilities of employees, employee benefits and services, separations, personnel records and orientation, training and education. This is supplemented by a 60-page memorandum of understanding with a union of official reporters. The reporters and recorders who work in the state courts of Michigan recently received a 48-page manual about such topics as certification of reporters, transcript formats, fees, ordering and filing transcripts, appellate procedures for reporters, and other topics. These two illustrations suggest that supervision has a technical and legal meaning to it in a location where the rules are spelled out in bureaucratic fashion. But there is another general and social side to supervision that deserves some attention.

During the work that followed the Certified Managing Reporter Module on Personnel Management in 1986, some of the persons who attended later researched and wrote what they learned about a good supervisor. The topic assigned was to develop a portrait of a good supervisor. The views of the reporters who attended covered a wide range of general characteristics of supervisor. Several said that a supervisor of reporters must know reporting, that a knowledge of the field is critical. But being armed with knowledge of reporting is just a start. A knowledge of the people who are to be supervised is helpful, and knowing a judge's requirements in reporting is vital. Others said that a knowledge of clients is very important in the assignment of reporters for deposition work. The knowledge bank of a managing reporter is beginning to bulge a little already. Many said that a supervisor must be fair, and must not play people against one another. Good communication and listening skills are a must for a managing reporter. One reporter wrote: rule with your head, but have a heart; be compassionate and understanding of the full life of the persons being supervised. Finally, most concluded that supervisors cannot please everyone all the time, so as a consequence they must prepare themselves for handling disagreement, disappointment, and discouragement. In all of the portraits of a good supervisor, there was a demand for realistic, humane behavior. Since the writers of these nine papers, Ellen V. Corbett, Linda Staklinski, Constance Goodner, Susan Gillette, Michael Wierzbicki, Jean Brdey, Karen Carney, Regis Taylor, and Marguerite Stebbins have a total of many, many years of supervising reporters, their views are particularly significant. There is a strong feminine view of supervision that reminds one of a nurturing activity, an activity of supervision that strives to allow people to get the best out of themselves at all times. And these supervisors are not dealing with vague generalities or grandiose theory; they manage in the day-to-day, nitty-gritty world of reporting. They are all reporters and have risen through the ranks, but they understand the decision making required in sending reporter A out to report job X. They seem to be highly receptive to the thoughts, ideas, and feelings of others, but each expressed a need for firmness and fairness in making timely decisions.

Along with this view of supervision it is important to develop the awareness that many others are concerned about the problems of supervision, leadership, training, job environment, predicting work satisfaction, and guiding vocational choice. In addition to the resources mentioned before, the work of John B. Miner is significant (Miner 1980). In his *Theories of Organizational Behavior*, Miner has evaluated a wide range of research on organizational behavior. Solid chapters summarize the need hierarchy theory, achievement motivation theory, motivation-hygiene theory, equity theory, expectancy theory, goal setting theory and management by objectives, behavior modification and operant learning theory, job characteristic theory of work redesign, theory X, and theory Y. Three areas summarized relate to leadership research: contingency theory, path-goal theory, and decision tree and related types of theories (Miner 1980). This research monograph is mentioned to encourage readers to pursue questions and issues about the theories of organizational behavior using new sources. As Miner suggests, however, "To stop with the field of organizational behavior is to know only half of what the functioning of organizations is all about" (Miner 1980, 417). Structures, processes, and environments of organizations are other major areas where managers could pursue their research and practice interests.

EMPLOYEE SELECTION AND PROFESSIONALISM

A suitable conclusion to this chapter on personnel management for managing court reporters is to think of professionalism in working with other reporters. Selecting reporters to work with a firm or to join a group in a courthouse is a significant step. Eileen Hyatt, in the introduction to this book, said, "Quality starts with hiring the best people, people who are committed to the same standard as yours." Hiring is extremely important, and the guidelines she suggests support the idea of looking for a sense of professionalism in potential colleagues. Other reporters in the introduction stress this same theme. Leonard Sayles urges us to give some serious thought to what is meant by professionalism. He believes that learning a professional approach is one key toward job satisfaction (Sayles 1985). Professionals differ from nonprofessionals. First, professionals have a sense of responsibility to clients. They do not think of clients as objects or money, nor do they say anything just to please or manipulate clients. Professionals, according to Sayles, exercise a quality of judgment that is not self-serving and that brings broad insight and calm judgment. Emotionalism does not drive a professional's judgment but could in fact hurt it. Professionals are not just technicians applying a fixed body of techniques supplemented by an occasional glance at a new trade publication.

The contradictions, trade-offs, and risks in making decisions are known by professionals and communicated to clients. As Sayles says: "Real professionals have learned that excellence isn't an end state" (Sayles 1985, 10). This applies to managing reporters who have to strive continuously to exercise a professional spirit in the reporter profession.

4

Financial Management for Managing Reporters

Next to people, money is a central topic for any manager. Financial controls are powerful but are *not* the only source of power in an organization. Money expressed as the profit motive is central for reporters in private firms, and for public reporters who have a private practice. Since the entrepreneurial spirit cuts across the public–private dimension of the reporting profession, this topic of financial management appeals to a wide spectrum of reporters. Official reporters care about private finance—they have a private life. Freelance reporters care about public finance if they work for governments from time to time. Managing reporters in either group find themselves deeply enmeshed with finances and financial problems.

Every aspect of an organization has an obvious financial angle. Personnel need salaries, fringe benefits, and resources to function. They also need automobiles, phones, copiers, and other tools. Marketing requires money for advertising and public relations. Technology calls for money. Money is an inescapable necessity anywhere in reporter organizations. The owners of reporting firms have capital funds tied up in real and personal property used by the firm, and they expect a return on their investment called profit.

The economic environment of a reporter firm is critical to its functioning. The competitive climate, the presence of capital to borrow for operational or other needs, the availability of accountants and auditors, and the availability of investment advisors and others who help to shape the long-range financial planning in a reporter firm are critical. Tax planning requires financial and legal advice. The economic climate is sometimes deeply affected by the political climate as it impacts on budgets for public services. Reporting in the public sector is a public service and it is caught up with the politics related to reducing taxes and public expenditure. Reporters are influenced by the economy—by inflation, depression, unemployment—along with everyone else in society. The financial side of managing is not easy to grasp, or to influence, through management action. Nonetheless, managers are expected to be knowledgeable and adept in financial management.

For the analysis of financial management, a convenient approach is to break the subject into three parts: business finance, personal finance, and public finance. Business finance explores money management strategies related to pricing and billing for services, to salary and fringe benefits for employees, to taxes on the business, and to financial information for managing. Personal finance is directed more toward strategies for investments, taxes, insurance, and estate planning. Public finance is directed toward a better insight into public budgets, and primarily their execution in the judicial branch. Business and personal finance are directed more toward free-lance reporters, whereas public finance affects official reporters. But there is a mutual interest in all parts of the reporter profession in economic health of the entire profession. This is the professional bottom line.

BUSINESS FINANCE

Some of the financial management questions for a managing reporter are:

- Are we charging enough for our services as reporters?
- Do we have enough money in the checking account to write a check?
- We want to buy a new CAT system. How would we pay for it? Or should we lease it?
- It will soon be April 15 and the tax men in the federal, state, and local government are waiting for tax returns. What should we do?
- We don't have enough income this month to pay employees—what will the bank want to know when we ask to borrow money?
- What can we set aside for retirement under tax laws?
- A new building for our firm would be wonderful. Could we afford it?
- Three months have gone by and there is still no payment for the transcript. What do we do?
- How do we make sure that our financial books and records are truthful, accurate, and timely.

These questions call into play all the paper trappings of financial management: business checking accounts, expense files, billing procedures, receipts, bank statements, accounting records and books, and more.

Money Management

Reporting is a personal service that must be priced and sold. Once sold, it must be paid for. Pricing reporter services and collecting all the bills submitted are two sides to the same task of financial management. The pricing of reporter service must cover overhead, taxes, and a profit. Overhead includes office expenses, travel, entertainment, stationery, and supplies. This ranges, in service businesses, "between 30 and 40 percent of gross annual revenue" (Creedy 1980, 47). If you plan to bill your time at 200 billable days a year, you can begin to distribute your overhead at 30% to 40% of gross salary along with 20%–25% of gross salary for taxes, leaving you 40%–50% of gross salary for net salary and profit (Creedy 1980, 48). Formulas to calculate billable days per year are common in service businesses (Creedy 1980). Time value computed by the minute is also available (Henry 1985, 15–16).

A special aspect of pricing for reporters is the page rate for transcripts. The fees for transcripts are frequently established by law, and the law is exceedingly specific in some states. For example, margins, headings and other format details are specified. These statutory rates change only with political pressure on governing bodies. This is a potential source of difficulty in pricing during inflationary periods. The tendency will be for page rates to lag behind inflation, forcing reporters to work at a potential loss.

Another aspect to pricing service is the forecasting of income, both total, or gross income, and net income levels based upon certain hourly charges. The more income desired, the higher the hourly, or other, charge to clients. Fixed expenses, like the electrical power or pieces of paper used in a month, are thrown into the formula to forecast income (Creedy 1980, 52).

Once reporting service is intelligently priced in a particular market, charges for the service still must be collected from clients. There are varieties of experiences that need to be examined in detail. Most of us have experienced credit policies applied to us by banks, credit card companies, stores with charge accounts, car companies, and mortage associations. These same credit policies are important when reporters establish client relationships and then bill for their services (Henry 1985, 103–119; Creedy 1980, 45–68; Borgmann 1986; Gilman 1984; Rogner 1985). It is important to be clear-minded in the development of credit policies in any service, and this is particularly true for those reporters who are *not* paid on a regular basis by well-known clients. Strategies that lead to intelligent pricing of services and to maximum receipt of billed hours reduce risks in two significant areas of money management. One risk is that a reporter is not billing realistically, and the other risk is that a reporter is not collecting what is owed in a timely manner. These policies, it would seem, are keystones in the arch of developing sound financial practices in a free-lance firm. Obviously, both pricing and billing are not static activities, but require continual review.

Salary and fringe benefit management for firm employees is a vital area where a firm's management can be concerned and can express that concern to employees by continual attention. Private salary surveys in a locality, use of consultants to develop data about salary and fringe benefit packages, and concerted attention will demonstrate fairness. This aspect of money management is a source of constant change due to inflation, expansion of fringe benefits, changes in tax laws, and other factors. Paying attention to salaries is an important financial activity of managing reporters.

Tax strategies are part of financial management. Everyone knows how frequently Congress has changed federal income tax laws. A third of gross income may be impacted by taxes. Two business areas seem significant enough to mention briefly. Buying a building to house a reporting service and renting unused space to others is a tax strategy used by some reporters to take advantage of tax laws. The other tax strategy is CAT equipment acquisition that can be depreciated and expensed to reduce taxable income for a few years. These two strategies are as permanent as any reasonable and necessary business expense under the tax codes. Reducing taxes is an important part of tax strategy (Henry 1985, 157–186).

Risks of loss are always present, so it is important to protect a business with insurance in cases of malpractice, business interruption, crime, and fire. There is no way a single business could survive for long without insurance. Operating an automobile in business is just one example of exposure to significant financial risks. Contingency theory welcomes insurance because it is a rational, cost-effective way of dealing with uncertainties.

The financial side of a professional practice requires data. Income and expense statements, net worth statements to banks for a loan, pricing, billing for accounts receivable, salary administration, and taxes all depend on the quality of the data in the firm. Microcomputers are coupled with accounting software in some of the larger reporting firms in the nation. For example, Eileen Hyatt and Karen Carney mentioned their systems in the introduction to this book. The need for accounting services raises the question of the type of certified public accountant desired. Whether you or your accountant use the financial data, the aims of financial management are to develop enough data at the least cost so that the firm is operating on realistic financial terms with data that is not too vague, too old, too confusing, or too ambiguous (Henry 1985, 127–139). All data have limits of utility in addition to the costs of data collection. Financial management takes these factors into account.

Special financial analyses are part of managing a firm's money. A good illustration of financial analysis is provided by Jill Wilson in her article, "What Will CAT Cost Me?" (Wilson 1985). Examining a variety of costs, projecting over a future period, examining cash flow and after-tax income, developing cost-per-page data—all of these tools of financial analysis are helpful in making a financial decision for the reporting firm.

Business finance for the managing reporter becomes a constant review of sound financial information that will help to answer the questions raised at the outset of this material: will the checkbook balance, are the debts paid, are the tax laws obeyed and is the firm paying the least amount of tax required by law, are clients paying bills promptly, did we make a profit, and are the accounting records honest and truthful? These are important questions and aims of wise financial management in a reporting firm or in a solo practice.

PERSONAL FINANCE

It is simple to separate a person from his participation in a corporate person or from his role in a partnership with others in a reporting firm. It is not simple to separate a person from a sole proprietorship where the business consists of that person and perhaps one or more employees. The reason for noting the confusion of identity is that it affects free-lance reporters who may have a range of financial concerns that involve their reporter business, but that also affect their personal tax return every year. The dividing line between business expense and personal expense is almost a daily issue for such reporters. Recognizing this division of expenses and its complexity in financial management is important, especially when tax audit time arrives and the review process by government agents requires that nondeductible personal expenses be distinguished from business expenses that are deductible from gross income. Gradually we all learn to make clear lines of division in our records for tax purposes. What is needed here is to separate business financial issues we have reviewed from personal issues of finance. NSRA has been offering a wealth of important insight in recent years in the area of personal finance.

Investment strategies require knowledge that is offered by expertise of varying quality from many sources such as bankers, stock brokers, investment counselors, accountants, attorneys, and insurance brokers. This is an area where "buyer beware" is an excellent starting point. An informed consumer probably takes courses in investment at a local college, receives a variety of periodicals, studies books by some leading authorities, and practices his knowledge in the investment field. The *National Shorthand Reporter* publishes articles that attempt to interest the professional in the area of personal finance. Titles of various articles suggest the range of interest: "A Bit of Background on Tax-Favored Retirement Plans" (February 1986), "Making The Most of Your IRA Assets" (February 1986), "Money Sense I & II" (March 1981), "Planning an Investment Portfolio" (February 1980), "Tax Tips" (February 1980), "Money Management for Two-Income Couples" (February 1986), and "Fixing Up Your Finances" (February 1985). These articles are designed to assist reporters in the achievement of personal goals such as achieving and sustaining suitable income, investing surplus wisely, and planning an estate. Personal investing requires time and attention. In sole proprietorships of reporters, the issues of business finance and personal financial management are blended in a predictable way. One intelligent resource for reporters to review is Donald L. Henry's "The Profitable Professional Practice" (Henry 1985). After developing a range of business issues for a practicing professional in 16 chapters, Henry concludes with a chapter devoted to a professional practitioner's investment and retirement program. Although information about the 1986 tax reform act is not included, Henry's book offers advice on federal taxes, employee pension plans, Keogh plans, IRA's, money market funds, treasury notes and bonds, treasury bills, bonds, and other topics. Henry recognizes that business and personal financial management are different sides of a professional who is attempting to manage his or her financial affairs.

PUBLIC FINANCE

Most official reporters probably do not have any involvement in the public financing of the court in which they work. In fact, the remoteness of financial issues from the work of the official reporter is one of the most striking comparisons between a reporter in the public arena and a reporter who works in a private firm. Judges who have come on the bench from a successful private practice will also experience this same remoteness from money issues that may well be handled by county officials, presiding judges and court administrators. Both the judge and the reporter will not be centrally involved in the elaborate financial management activities in government. Nevertheless, it is important that official reporters become acutely aware of the budgeting process in government. Official reporters may express effective financial management by lobbying a legislature to modify legal and fiscal constraints that are financially dysfunctional for reporters.

Public budgets are developed about six months to a year before they are finally adopted a few months before the start of the next fiscal year. The distant horizon of the public budget is quite different from that of private finance. While a financial manager in a government may be auditing a prior fiscal year, he may also be authorizing an expenditure in the current budget year and planning a budget for future year. Dealing with 36 months of data is not unusual in most public financial management environments. The budgeting process is cycled: it begins, it develops, it is halted, it is executed for a year, and then it is audited. If one is dealing with three budget cycles at once, budget talk can be confusing. Before plunging into public financial issues, it is helpful to know what stage the budget cycle is in and the year of the budget in question.

The main items of concern to official reporters are: the salary of the reporter, the deductions from the salary for social security and taxes, the deductions for employee-paid insurance, retirement and other programs, and the transcript billing process. A change in any one of these items is a group event for most reporters. For a few unionized reporters it is a union bargaining process. But there are other benefits for public reporters: space, heat, light, parking, janitorial service, office equipment and furniture, telephones, copiers, and other needs are provided. An alteration in any of these items in the budget requires group attention. The travel expenses of reporters may be reimbursed. Unless a reporter is the only reporter in the courthouse, the issue of comparability and equity among reporters usually requires joint decision making. In some courthouses this decision process has been developed, while in others it remains to be developed.

Financial resources for reporters come from public treasuries of the following governments: the federal government (for over a thousand federal reporters), 50 state governments (for reporters who are paid salaries and transcript fees), 3,000 county governments (for reporters who are county employees on a limited basis), and some cities (for reporters who may be part of a city government court structure). Each of these governments has its own budget process, budget cycle, financial requirements, and audit demands. There is no way to generalize about the nature of these governments and their financial managements, since little is known about the reporter's involvement in this management process.

The following salary information for official reporters was published in 1984 (Kotzan 1984). Table 2 shows a wide range of public reporters' salaries because jurisdictions vary in the rules relating to free-lance work, transcript production and per page fees. These data are restricted to stenotype operators, since they form the dominant group offering services to governments.

In the states not listed in the table—such as Alaska, California, Florida, Louisiana, and Texas—salaries vary by county, and data were presumably not available. In some other missing states, the information provided about the number of reporters or salary was not complete. Thus a comparison did not seem appropriate. Over 200 pen shorthand reporters were also excluded. CAT, stenomask, and audio recording personnel were also excluded because they are fringe populations of the main group in government. Federal reporters were also missing from this table.

Transcript fees are a common source of additional income for government reporters. For about 30 jurisdictions the most common transcript fee range in 1983 was $1.26 to $2.00 for each original page (Kotzan 1984). Of these jurisdictions 15 were in the $1.76 to $2.00 range. However, the variability of transcript fee arrangements is so great that there is no convenient way to summarize it further. While the page rate may not sound like much, millions of transcripts of civil and criminal proceedings are produced every year. At 2,000 hours a year, a core of 2,225 reporters has 4.45 million hours of available service. Not all is devoted to transcript production, however. In very significant, long, and complex trials, a 10,000-page transcript is not unknown. Transcripts of this length are rare, but they represent the extreme end of production. Many proceedings are five-minute affairs, and such a transcript may be just a few pages. These extremes illustrate the range of demands that individual reporters must be able to meet through transcript activity. This means that reporters are required to serve in court during regular court hours and perform transcript work whenever it can be done—

Table 2
Number and Annual Salary of Court Reporting Personnel (Summer of 1983)

State	No. of Reporters	Annual Salary or Salary Range (dollars)
1. Alabama	71	18,955
2. Arizona	93	16,704 - 30,867
3. Colorado	109	16,464 - 28,128
4. Connecticut	92	20,643 - 24,597
5. Delaware	5	25,000
6. Dist. of Columbia	35	20,256 - 38,185
7. Hawaii	42	21,800 - 31,932
8. Idaho	29	24,000
9. Illinois	510	11,264 - 26,496
10. Iowa	115	15,450 - 25,850
11. Kansas	113	20,196 - 27,084
12. Kentucky	27	13,200 - 20,484
13. Massachusetts	38	22,524 - 28,667
14. Missouri	108	24,030
15. Nebraska	42	23,248
16. Nevada	32	20,000
17. New Hampshire	16	22,118 - 26,775
18. New Jersey	214	15,709 - 34,000
19. New Mexico	76	25,000 - 35,000
20. North Carolina	69	15,612 - 22,488
21. North Dakota	24	27,360
22. Oregon	81	21,456 - 27,348
23. Rhode Island	36	17,418 - 20,111
24. South Carolina	18	22,439
25. Tennessee	24	7,500 - 11,700
26. Utah	29	23,698 - 31,173
27. Vermont	14	19,000 - 24,000
28. Wisconsin	211	20,218 - 31,219
	2273	

at night, on weekends, and during holidays. Most transcripts must be produced within a time frame of a few months as established by state law, court rule, or a combination of both. Increasingly, these time frames are being carefully monitored and enforced by appellate courts.

Managing reporters should be aware of public financial management trends. One basic fact about judicial branch financing in the United States is that it is mixed financing, with states and counties providing the dollar resources. Some states have modified their judicial articles in the last two decades to offer greater state financing of the judicial budget, thereby reducing the amount of county tax needed. This type of shift has been labeled "unified court budgeting," but the label covers a set of political, social, and organizational processes that are very traumatic. New York, for example has experienced such a change that it is described in some detail by one of the insiders, Ronald Stout (Stout 1986). Reporters in official positions who are caught up in these mini-revolutions should be aware of the ramifications and be prepared to deal with them. The proposers of unified budgets are motivated by political aims as are those who are content with the political status quo. Ensuring that the reporting function is not harmed by such change is a major responsibility of a managing reporter in a public court system.

In the public arena, official reporters will face increased pressure from court managers, judges, county and state budget officials, and others who want to dig deeply into the costs of reporting and analyze the benefits. An analytical tool commonly used in the public organization is a cost-benefit analysis. A cost-benefit analysis was applied to word processing by the National Center for State Courts (National Center for State Courts 1984). Cost-benefit analysis has also been applied extensively to official reporters in a 1979 Connecticut study, a 1985 Kentucky study, and a 1986 Maryland study. (National Center for State Courts 1979, 1985, and 1986). These three studies examined fixed and variable costs, and tangible and intangible benefits. Some of these reports use a "cost score" which treats cost calculations in a simple form, representing relative orders of magnitude to avoid a bewildering array of numbers of actual costs. A numerical weight of one to ten is assigned to personnel costs, transcript fees, appellate record review, facility changes, equipment, supplies, and storage. These numerical figures are then weighted and totaled. Benefits are also assigned a numerical weight from one to ten and these numbers are applied to record accuracy, record reliability, obtrusiveness, transcript accuracy, transcript timeliness, ease of review, dependence on in-court operator for transcription, policy flexibility, enhancement capacity, suitability for education, and productivity. These weights are then totaled comparing various types of reporting.

Managing reporters who want to use cost-benefit analysis must comprehend two important points. First, the analytical power of a cost-benefit analysis such as that applied by The National Center for State Courts in the three jurisdictions studied depends critically upon the definitions assigned to the scheme of weighting. Second, the weights assigned to numbers, the numbers selected, and the logic behind such choices deserves precise attention. What begins as a financial analytical tool—cost-benefit analysis—frequently becomes another type of analytical tool that is increasingly judgmental without reference to cost. This is a more dangerous form of analysis because it is cloaked with numbers that are chosen in an arbitrary manner and thus have no basis in real cost analysis as it is applied in industry and business where time, materials, and expenses are totaled. The result is that conclusions of such studies are certainly no better than the quality of the analysis of real costs and real benefits. In other words, cost-benefit analysis can be used in this manner to reach *any* conclusion one desires.

While such cost-benefit analysis appears to be analytical in nature, the real question the managing reporter must ask is: How genuine is the analysis? The admonition is: take time to study in great detail the methods chosen for cost studies of any kind. Cost-benefit analysis is just one of the tools from systems theory, which has its place and its limits *if* properly applied.

In closing this chapter, please note that organizational theories—systems theory, contingency, human relations, and bureaucracy—are still with us. Financial management cuts across all the theoretical perspectives while each theory contributes some deeper understanding to the practice of financial management. The theory–practice nexus was illustrated in this chapter using a variety of examples.

5

Marketing Management for Managing Reporters

> The shorthand reporter shall be truthful and accurate when making public statements or when advertising the reporter's qualifications or the services provided.
>
> NSRA Code of Professional Conduct 1986

In the United States, everyone slowly but surely becomes bombarded with enough commercial marketing, especially in direct mail, newspapers, and television, that an immune system develops. Remote controls on television sets have muting buttons which reduce the din of the marketing noise to zero. Our eyes search between the ads on each page of the newspaper trying to spot the true news. Few societies are blessed or cursed with this daily feast of advertising and public relations backed by billions of dollars of expenditures. Amidst the shouting and clamor of the general market place, there are quiet, discreet sources of promotion where reporters and lawyers hang out. These narrow avenues of promotion are important with regard to the marketing of professional reporter services.

PROFESSIONAL SERVICE MARKETING

In Chapter 1, evidence and arguments were developed concluding that reporters are conducting a profession of reporting. If we understand what reporters do, we also understand that the most complex tasks do require very high levels of knowledge, talent, and continual learning. Once again, the professional nature of the reporter's work is important in assessing the marketing of such services. The 1986 NSRA code of ethics provision quoted at the beginning of this chapter is the bottom line: standards of honesty, accuracy, and fairness must prevail in the promotion of a professional reporting service. Since 1978, the legal profession has shown that advertising the prices of legal services has begun to revolutionize advertising and public relations for that profession. Since reporters work so closely with the legal profession, the experience of lawyers merits a brief review.

Before 1977, Frederick C. Moss indicates that lawyers marketed their practices by informal means—by joining social clubs, political organizations, and business and civic groups (Moss 1986). Television and newspaper ads for lawyers services were not considered ethical behavior. Bar-recommended fee schedules were the norm. In 1977, the United States Supreme Court heard *Bates* v. *State Bar of Arizona*, 433 U.S. 350, in which two attorneys were sanctioned by the bar (one year suspension from practice) for running a printed advertisement quoting standard prices for legal services in such matters as uncontested divorces. The Supreme Court split, but a widely quoted statement by Justice Blackmun set the tone for a new view of advertising legal professional services. The court found that the free speech provisions of the First Amendment to the United States Constitution protected the commercial speech of the two lawyers in Arizona who were seeking clients through ads:

> Commercial speech serves to inform the public availability, nature and prices of products and services, and this performs an indispensable role in the allocation of resources in a free enterprise system.

The *Bates* case and others made it obvious that attitudes toward marketing the legal profession had changed in the Supreme Court. Lori Andrews remarked that a salesman may have been born: "Now that the law is no longer a rich man's profession and clients, too, come from all social strata, the method of matching up lawyers and clients is moving from the country clubs into the mass media" (Andrews 1979, 85). Clients found that availability, reputation, experience, specialty in law, price or fee, and helpfulness at consultation—in that order—were the critical criteria for the selection of a lawyer (Andrews 1979, 28).

In less than a decade since *Bates*, the legal profession is taking law firm marketing practices out of the closet (Moss 1986, 602). Moss concluded his extensive analysis by stating: "The legal profession and American society now stand on the brink of a new era in law practice marketing" (Moss 1986, 694). In a thorough review of marketing ethics for lawyers, Moss examined in fine detail what is misleading in advertising about lawyers: their record of past performances, reputations, biographical information, endorsements and testimonials, puffing and self-laudation, claims of expertise and specialization, statements about fees, their logos, illustrations, pictures, music, lyrics, and dramatizations. There are some undignified, garish aspects that need to be considered seriously. Moss examined the promotion of referrals, especially with lay intermediaries. Promoting media exposure—being in the news, creating news releases, appearing on broadcast media, speaking at seminars and conferences and direct solicitation by calls, mailings, and hiring public relations firms—was another aspect analyzed by Moss. These inevitable changes in law practice marketing began as a dramatic change in the 1977 *Bates* case with the protection of lawyers' commercial speech in promoting their services to clients. In all probability, this change in attitude toward promotion in the legal profession will affect the entire reporter profession.

Geoffrey Hazard, former director of the American Bar Foundation, and now a professor at Yale University, along with two colleagues, offered a strong support for advertising what they call "standardizable legal service." In a 1983 article these authors segmented the legal market into "individualized service and standardized service." A person who needs a lawyer for individualized service has a high risk of loss, and personal knowledge about a potential lawyer's reputation would be the key to hiring the lawyer. Such high-risk cases involve vast estates, large security issues, mergers of major corporations, and serious liability issues in tort or criminal cases. On the other hand, standardizable service is a low-risk, routine production, where low cost is important to clients and advertising would increase the numbers of potential clients. These low-risk cases are uncontested divorces, simple wills for small sums, and routine collection litigation, for example. The authors argue that the "public interest bar" that has come into being since World War II has a clinical approach to lawyering and sees advertising as a very favorable means to reach large numbers of people. The authors argue, "Of course, the practice of law manifestly is both a profession and a business, and a highly competitive business at that" (Hazard, Pearce, and Stempel 1983, 1112). In the case of standardizable service, they support broader use of lawyer advertising. The arguments parallel those made in Chapter 1 of this book: that reporters are both professionals and business people. The marketing issues are remarkably parallel in both professions. Reporters could even segment their market in a way that resembles this.

Sometimes the obvious needs to be mentioned so that it becomes clearer that developing a reporter firm is a difficult marketing feat. A physical display of reporting services can be offered only after a transcript is prepared, unless real-time translation is at work in a CAT system. Demonstrations of service are not easy to perform although they can be managed. Warranties and guarantees do not apply to professional service in the way that they apply to a toaster, for example. There is no patent protection. There are no meaningful samples and there is not much one can tie a pretty bow around and call a package of reporter services. As one thoughtful observer noted: "services are said to be intangible, not durable, cannot be tested, production and consumption must be simultaneous and the user has to participate in the production of the service" (A. Wilson 1984, 8). While this quotation is not completely accurate for reporting, it at least suggests the difficulty of expressing to clients what a job actually involves. Marketing of professional services must overcome these difficult barriers of proof in order to build trust.

COMPETITION IN REPORTING ENVIRONMENTS

Environments

Reporting services are concentrated in the 250 major urban areas of the United States, but such services exist rather broadly across the entire nation. The local legal cultures that exist are bounded by a county, and there are about 3,000 counties in the nation. The environments for a reporter vary from Los Angeles County or Cook County, to a rural county in western Tennessee. The amount of legal business, the numbers of practicing lawyers, the presence of one or more courthouses, the numbers, types, experience, and professional longevity of other reporters, the numbers of reporter firms, and the economic wealth of the area must be taken into account when assessing the competitive strategies that make sense in a particular locality. This is the first stage of marketing analysis.

One environmental factor that affects a reporter's work directly is a more accelerated method for processing court cases and for appealing cases. Depositions in the pretrial state and the trial stages are being faced with shorter and shorter deadlines, and some law firms are beginning to request electronic media such as diskettes in place of paper depositions. The pressure from the courts to avoid litigation delays requires lawyers and reporters to work much more rapidly than in past decades. The CAT technology, with rapid transcript production, invites clients to shorten reporter time allowances. These conditions will affect all reporters serving the law firms in a community. Some insurers and law firms request a bidding process for multiparty litigation where there is major litigation in the offing. The free-lance reporter is confronted by such an competitive environment and must learn to manage within it.

Managing Tasks Environments

According to systems theory, organizations depend on exchanges with their environments in order to survive. Organizations have boundaries and managers span the boundaries of the organization, by setting and resetting the boundaries of the organization (Scott 1987, 181). Reporter firms are formed and develop, and some die. Law firms experience this same fluidity—partners join and split over time. Death, resignation, retirement, and other factors cause the reporter organization to undergo change. In the process of change, the boundaries of the reporter firm expand, recede, or stay the same at different times. Most important for competitive management actions are what have been identified as *buffering* and *bridging* strategies (Scott 1981, 188).

Buffering strategies

To protect the core technology of a reporter firm—that is, the production of reporter notes and transcripts to conform with client demands—managers act as buffers by using five strategies: coding, stockpiling, leveling, forecasting, and growth. Let me try to illustrate each of these strategies in a reporter firm. Classifying clients according to difficulty of reporting tasks and then assigning appropriately experienced reporters to those tasks is a *coding* activity which assures smooth operations. *Stockpiling* involves allowing transcript orders to pile up to make a larger unit of work which can be be done at a slower time. *Leveling* of demand involves scheduling maintenance service on CAT equipment in down periods when reporting demand is slack. Shifting transcript work to times of the day, week, or month when demand for notetaking is lower is a *leveling* technique. *Forecasting* is a way to estimate the demand, which could drop to zero on days when all of the judges and lawyers in a state are attending an annual professional conference. Finally, *growth* is a strategy which allows the organization to reach a size where it has more leverage and variety in its environment and more clients with greater diversity of demand, so that the technical core can operate more freely and consistently without disturbances in demand from outside.

Bridging Strategies

Enhancing the security of an organization in its environment requires bridging strategies that span an organization's boundaries. For example, the interdependence of reporter firms and their uncertain relations with one another are partly the result of two or more firms competing for the same business from the same set of law firms. The competitive reporter firms can *bargain* with one another to get the business of the local law firm. The local law firm can play one reporter firm off against the other to develop alternative suppliers of services. Bargaining is a strategy all the players can use. *Contracting* with suppliers by use of retainers or other long-term contractual relationships, say on multiparty litigation, is another stabilizing competitive strategy used by reporting firms. *Cooptation* is incorporating representatives of external groups into the decision-making or advisory structure of a group or organization. Reporter firms call in management consultants, lawyers, accountants, and insurance agents to assist them in developing competitive approaches. *Joint ventures* commonly unite two or more reporting firms to handle litigation depositions in several cities simultaneously. *Mergers* of organizations arise to integrate vertically up the supply chain, to merge horizontally like businesses, or to diversify business. Reporter firms do merge. *Associations*—such as the associations of shorthand reporters—of local, county, state, and national organizations are well known. Associations indirectly influence competitive practices, especially in approaches taken toward competitive technology. *Governmental* and *institutional* linkages are two other bridging strategies used by organizations. For example, reporters bridge the working world by accepting speaking engagements with the National Judicial College or with the university community. Reporters use both bridging and buffering strategies in the competive stances and actions of their firms.

PRACTICE DEVELOPMENT OR GROWTH

The idea that marketing is for business and that developing a practice is for a profession is a twisted, unsound approach. Perhaps one could better argue that the business side of a professional practice is a secondary activity that supports the main professional activity. No one goes to law school to learn how to classify and file legal materials, but lawyers are doing this constantly, with help from their staff. No physician goes to medical school because he or she wants to keep a set of medical records or accounting books to satisfy the IRS. And no reporter goes into reporting just for the sake of marketing his or her services in order to build a firm. Legal advice, medical practice, and reporting services are the main professional services clients want and need. The offices and settings from which professional service is delivered are important bases from which development of a practice can proceed.

The development of a professional practice involves everything a managing reporter does in buffering and bridging strategies in the areas of personnel, finance, and technology, but in this chapter, the primary focus is on marketing strategies for the development of the firm. For example, having something to say in reporter presentations is a matter of developing material. While reporters are the listeners in legal proceedings, there comes a time in marketing when they must talk about their reporting services. Selecting the media and the message to deliver to targeted people is the central purpose of marketing. To expand a reporting firm, to replace lost clients, and to retain clients are interrelated tasks of survival in a competitive environment where inflation, technology, and client attitudes are in flux.

One element of developing a reporter practice is to create a client-centered practice (A. Wilson 1984, 19). Sensing the needs of law firms, responding to their inquiries, and seeking out chances to provide new services are three ways of acting in a client-centered manner. If law firms ask for different types of reporting technology—say video deposition—the client-centered firm would consider and probably offer the service or see that reliable service is provided in some manner. Practice development requires planning in a variety of fields like these. Deciding on the range of services, understanding clients' needs, comprehending how reporters are selected by clients, indentifying potential new clients, working more fully with whatever referral systems exist in the area of practice desired, and using both personal and impersonal means of contacting clients are combined elements in a strategy of marketing (A. Wilson 1984; Henry 1985).

Images

The field of marketing is sometimes accused of creating false images of services and products through advertising and public relations techniques that stretch the truth. The name for this deception is puffery. While this may be true, we all create images of ourselves that persist in the mind and memory of others. Robert Burns, the Scottish poet, said it would be a wonderful gift to see ourselves as others see us. Managing reporters need to be aware of the importance of the images and the perceptions portrayed by their firms. In the introduction to this book, several managing reporters expressed a deep concern that their business and professional images be taken seriously. Wilson has identified at least three images to consider (A. Wilson 1984, 141). A *current* image is the way a firm is seen by different publics. This is the objective image. The *mirror* image is the way a firm thinks it is seen by different publics. The mirror image may or may not be accurate. The *wish* image is the way a firm would like to be seen by its different publics. People who refer reporting business to a firm have one image. Clients who find a lack of punctuality in the fulfilment of that firm's appointments and deadlines have still another image. Lasting impressions are built through these images. An unfair fee can sour a client unless a firm has a method of exploring such issues with clients. Complaints about the quality of service can be handled by ignoring them or by exploring them in detail. Images cannot be avoided in service businesses. Having an image that is competent, well established, friendly, fair, and reliable is decidedly better than having an image of being unfair, cold, difficult, too expensive, pompous, and constantly late. Image-making is more than mirrors. Those who are developing a practice must take images and perceptions into account.

EFFECTIVE COMPETITION FOR CLIENTS

Effective competition for clients does three important things for a reporting firm. Current clients are retained and satisfied, unless something very drastic (like bankruptcy, retirement, or death) happens to the client. New clients are attracted to replace lost clients and to ensure the growth of the firm. And finally, the firm grows financially and intellectually, and the size of its work force increases. The type and rate of growth depend upon the wishes of the firm's principals. Effectiveness measured by growth is not simply growth for growth's sake; in other words, bigger is not necessarily better in professional service organizations. But growth remains important. First, clients are lost and must be replaced. This growth is a fact of life. To measure effectiveness by growth is justified also by economies of scale so that all parts of the organization are fully used. If the organization becomes large enough, it has more planning capacity, it can set and achieve prices, it can regulate demand, and can more readily influence clients. A growing firm attracts new professionals who wish to hitch their futures to a rising star. "Growth embraces the organization's survival value, then, by providing a cushion, or slack, against organizational failure" (Pfeffer and Salancik 1978, 139). The three ways to measure success in competing for clients are:

1. Did the firm keep a large number of satisfied clients?
2. Did the firm attract new clients for replacement of lost clients and for growth?
3. Did the firm grow in the ways it wanted to grow?

Proposals for Service

Users of reporter services may request several reporter firms to submit written proposals that give details about the proposed reporter, the estimated cost, and the method of reporting to be used for a reporting job. Law firms, insurance firms, convention managers, government agencies, and others who use reporter services want to know in detail what can be expected from a reporter firm. Once a written response has been submitted by a reporter firm, there may be an opportunity to make an oral presentation to the user. If any stage of the proposal process requires sales foresight, it is the presentation stage, because at this stage other firms have usually been excluded for a variety of reasons such as cost, approach, staffing, or other problems. Here the experiences of watching the very best lawyers make their cases in court are now useful to a practicing reporter who must make a presentation to a law firm. There are many points to consider (Marcus 1986, 281–295).

Advertising

Advertising is best illustrated by a billboard. It is physical, direct, eye-catching, appealing, and succinct. You only need to glance at it to get the point. Public relations is different and is distinguished from advertising for reasons that are not entirely clear. Public relations is usually free publicity that generates good will. Giving a speech to a local civic group is an example of public relations—it is supposed to create good will toward the speaker. Marketing specialists use a mix of advertising and public relations to develop a practice. Bruce Marcus suggests that networking—joining organizations and golf clubs—used with newer tools from advertising and public relations should round out the complete marketing effort of a reporter firm (Marcus 1986, 69).

Advertising in print is found in yellow pages directories, in classified advertising and tombstone ads, in direct mailings, and in service and institutional ads. Broadcast ads are offered on radio or television. These different forms of advertising require very different formats that specialists in the field learn through study and experience. Marcus believes that direct mail may be the "most effective of all professional service marketing tools" (Marcus 1986, 109). Direct marketing is a rapidly growing field that includes direct mail, direct telephone marketing, and interactive television (Gosden 1985). A letter to clients that points toward solutions to problems is direct and can be used with phone calls and other forms of advertising. A newsletter is less personal but is used by some professional firms to keep clients interested and informed about trends, events, and changes in the field. Some experts classify newsletters as public relations vehicles. Accountants, for example, use the newsletter to help clients keep abreast of tax changes. There are many instances in which newsletters are a thoroughly professional vehicle to communicate to clients a professional concern and interest (Marcus 1986, 237–248).

The design and production of advertisements whether by direct mail, newsletters, or print or broadcast media are worth the careful attention of a managing reporter. Here the knowledge and skills of advertising professionals ensures that the money is well spent for quality image building. Printing terms are an art form themselves. Market analysis, message construction, and delivery are demanding and continual activities, not merely one-shot affairs. If marketing is started, there is a long period of development, testing, and planned use of materials that can span several years. Advertising expertise can help in making the right choices. Whether such experts are hired as staff or whether external agents are used is probably not relevant for most reporter firms because of their small size. Hiring an advertising firm could be considered a marketing strategy (Marcus 1986, 261–276).

Public Relations

The public relations phase of promotion starts with a letterhead that projects a distinctive impression, builds immediate recognition, and attracts favorable attention. Every reporter firm has a letterhead, and some may even have a logo or firm symbol on it. In the court reporter listing in the *National Shorthand Reporter* there is widespread concern for graphics in the reporter profession. Many firms have logos. The extent to which this distinctiveness is carried over into other materials that clients see and use is not so well known or obvious.

Making news for newspapers, broadcast media, trade journals, and magazines is creating publicity about any topic. The techniques are limited only by one's imagination. Press releases, feature material, press conferences, and by-line articles are used to create attention and draw it to the reporter firm. Another effective publicity technique involves speeches and seminars in which principals take part in a wide range of public relations activities where the firm is mentioned. Finally, newsletters, mentioned previously, brochures announcing capabilities of the firm, position papers, annual reports, and reprints of articles prepared by firm principals are further avenues of public relations.

Both advertising and public relations are worth pursuing for different reasons. For a direct customer approach, advertising is a controlled activity with a price. Public relations is usually free or low cost, but is less controlled and less direct. If a more subtle approach is needed, public relations is the avenue. In the professional service field, public relations is perhaps more traditional and acceptable, but there is every indication that advertising is significant for the future of professional groups. Free-lance reporter firms are directly in the pathway of these major trends in marketing management.

6

Technology Management for a Human Reporting Profession

THE SWAY OF TECHNOLOGY

In the latter part of the 1980s, there is a deep, widespread, and proud excitement in the reporter profession that reaches an emotional crescendo at the annual national meeting of the National Shorthand Reporters Association. The recent national meetings in Kansas City and Boston, for example, showed the explosive nature of the changes taking place in the profession, especially in the area of technology. For reporters, the displays of technology are very impressive and extensive. The way NSRA reporters feel about the new technology was expressed by Thomas F. Runfola (president, 1985–1986) in October, 1983:

> My profession stems from man's desire and necessity to preserve the happenings of yesterday and today for tomorrow. Computer-aided transcription will put a living, breathing, intelligent, efficient professional in your courtroom at reasonable cost. It's the mission of the National Shorthand Reporters Association to help our members do their jobs the best they can with the latest technology, in an efficient manner, while preserving the quality of justice for those using the legal system. . . . We are here offering you the technology of today and we believe, of tomorrow. (Runfola 1984, 29)

The feeling of being at the edge of the latest developments in technological improvements has given reporters a new confidence, eagerness, and inner strength to reach out and become agents of change in their profession. This enthusiasm can be best appreciated by looking at the numbers of reporters who willingly have adopted computer aided transcription systems, often at their own expense. In Chapter 1, the history of the CAT system from 1960–

1987 was presented. This table depicts the estimated adoptions by reporters of new CAT tecbnology:

Year	No. of Estimated Adoptions by Reporters
1960	Experimental period
1965	Experimental period
1970	Experimental period
1975	1 experimental—Philadelphia
1980	100 to 200
1987	5,000 to 7,000

These data illustrate that the reporter profession in 1980 was just waiting, itching to get its hands on new technology to improve the preparation of transcriptions of stenotype notes. The first adoptions took place primarily in the private sector of reporting. One estimate suggested that 90% of early adoptions until 1983 were in the free-lance reporter field (Runfola 1984). Since 1983, adoptions have continued on the private side and now have begun to rise among the official reporters. For example, Hawaii has been highly modernized in the field for many years. Federal court reporters are now adopting CAT technology on a widespread basis, but CAT has been used in the largest federal court, with the greatest transcript demand of any federal trial court, in the Southern District of New York since 1978, where about 200,000 pages of transcript were CAT-produced by mid–1984 (J. Wilson 1984, 31).

The attention of the reporters has been riveted on CAT technology and well it should be. However, adoption of CAT technology is *not* like taking a new medicine by mouth. You cannot swallow a CAT pill and wait for the results. Adoption of CAT technology—even for the solo practitioner—is an expensive, complex, time-consuming learning task. In a group practice, CAT adoption is even more complex. Later in this chapter these adoption processes will be examined in more detail.

With the almost breathless pace of change in the reporter field, many in the legal profession, on the bench, and elsewhere have not been fully aware of the dramatic changes in reporter technology. The purpose of this introduction to the chapter is to make certain that the "flavor" of change in the reporter profession is obvious. Things are very different in the reporter profession of today. Compared with 10 or 15 years ago, the reporter profession has indeed made a quantum leap toward the next century. It is axiomatic that when a profession embraces modern technology and fully exploits the technology the way reporters are doing now, there is a period of time when the rest of the world must catch up with the profession. Every profession experiences this cultural lag phenomenon in the world around it, and reporters are presently seeing the lag slowly disappear as knowledge of these changes in technology becomes more widespread. The future looks particularly fascinating for both the bench and the bar while they realize the tremendous new potential in the reporter profession.

REPORTERS MANAGING THEIR TOOLS AND TECHNOLOGY

The excitement of new technology is part of a bigger picture. Now is the time to develop message number five on technology as stated in Chapter 1 and as alluded to throughout the previous chapters. The main message is:

> Reporting is a human service that is evolving with a multitechnological base of support systems—audio, computers, video, word processing, optical scanning, electronic mail, and others.

This view of reporter activity states that reporting is a human service and technology is a supporting system. This perspective was developed in Chapter 1, and its arguments and the relevant evidence will not be repeated here. But no area of reporting is more critically impacted by this perspective than the technological aspect of managing reporters. However, there are two major sources of confusion about technology that need to be identified at the outset.

The first source of confusion about technology is that the users of the technology become identified so closely with it that they become an integral part of it. The people may even be subservient to the equipment. In the field of reporting the human reporter must be kept separate from the tools used to report. By way of analogy, surgeons are not necessarily identified with knives, hammers, saws, or more fancy electronic surgical gear like laser tools used in eye surgery or elaborate brain-scanning machines. Everyone recognizes that a surgeon uses tools, hands, and brain, and it is necessary that the links among the three be sound if the surgeon is to operate. Reporters, in the same way, use pencils, pens, erasers, paper, stenotype machines, typewriters, word processors, electronic mail, computer-assisted transcription systems, tape recorders, video recorders, cameras, monitors, steno-masks, personal computers, computer software, and the technologies and supplies associated with all of this equipment. If one confuses the tool with the user of the tools, a great disservice is done to understanding the real reporting world. The tendency is to confuse tools and tool users. This should not be allowed to happen. The aim is to be realistic, objective and sensible. Reporting is a human service first; using any number of tools, second. In reporting, the quality of a human reporter is much more important than the tool used.

The second source of confusion is the tendency to use computer technology as an excuse for failure. With all of the publicity and hyperactivity about the computer world, it has turned into a "gee-whiz" phenomenon. The razzle-dazzle world of the computer is impressive but is the result of excessive advertising. One has to get around all of that if one wants to be a realistic manager. Liking computers is not enough, and it is no protection to the profession of reporting to use the computer as a shield. The computer must be a useful tool for reporters on its own terms, not just because it is popular, or because it will stave off the use of other tools of reporting such as audio or video tape recorders. No lawyer or judge will allow a reporter to use computer failure to mask the failure of a human reporter whose responsibility it is to report accurately. By now, everyone knows the system acronym "gigo"— "garbage in, garbage out." The reporter is responsible for "garbage in" in any CAT system. The audio reporter is responsible for all of the "inaudibles" on the audio or video tapes—the total failure of audio or video systems to record what they are supposed to report. There is "garbage in" and "garbage out" in using pens, CAT systems, video tapes, or audio tapes. We have learned by now that human beings must master and manage machines to make them our servants rather than our masters. No tool used by a profession will shield from criticism directed at substandard performance. Would we excuse surgeons who cause unnecessary permanent injury by using dull knives or excessive drugs for surgery? The shoe fits in any profession in terms of expected standards of performance. Since reporting is a profession, reporters will be held to professional standards, which means that their tools provide no protection or excuse from "garbage in." That is the human side of reporting, but professional standards call attention to human frailty by insisting upon quality performance.

One of the latest sources on reporting techniques reinforces the need for reporters to become critically aware of the "garbage in" error syndrome:

> Machine shorthand writing for computer translation necessitates a highly refined machine shorthand theory oriented towards the highest quality first-pass translation by the computer. This requires *clean, conflict-free, consistent* machine shorthand outlines. High levels of concentration, consistency, and proficiency are required in writing for CAT. (Block 1986)

The burden of making CAT technology work is on the reporter profession. CAT, audio video, or any other tools are no better than the reporter who uses them. This is no great discovery; it is true in all professions and has been true since such expertise of reporting developed. Both the tool and its user have an equal place in the equation of change, but professional responsibility leaves final responsibility on the tool user, in this case, the reporter. No one condemns a tool manufacturer if a transcript is in error.

The second aspect of the main message is about the meaning of "multi-technological" base. The reporter of today may be comfortable with knowing and practicing a single form of reporting—say a stenotype CAT system.

The availability of video depositions, the need for some record in proceedings where a transcription is not needed or is rarely needed, the instances in which technology or tools can be varied to make a record of limited utility, all require that a reporter firm or even an individual reporter expand and vary services for clients or governments. The future reporter will, no doubt, concentrate on certain tools, but will, by necessity, become knowledgeable about all current and future tools of reporting. It is not farfetched to imagine a future reporter being able to offer any format or combination of formats by using tools in whatever combinations clients want. A record-making team could evolve if required for each ad hoc reporting need. There might be as many flavors of reporting as there are of ice cream. Daily copy is one of the flavors that reporters produce now.

The main message, "reporting is a human service that is evolving with a multitechnological base of support systems," should conjure up not a simple-minded point, but one that involves an entire reporter profession made up of thousands of people at various stages of development all trying to keep technology in an appropriate perspective. While it may be easy for a pen writer to keep CAT systems in perspective by never using them, once a reporter is under contract to purchase an expensive CAT system and is in the middle of training, there is a natural transformation of the interest of that person. For those who have been successful reporters for years and who mastered CAT several years ago, it is easy to keep CAT in perspective. But for many reporters coming into the profession, there is an awesome quality to computer technology. Sitting in a newcomer's chair, the perspective on technology is quite different. Such reporters need to gain a broad perspective on technology more quickly than experience permits, but they should not be overpowered by technology.

MANAGEMENT PERSPECTIVES

In *Managing New Office Technology*, Calvin Pava develops an organizational strategy that managers need to grasp fully (Pava 1983). The technological wizardry just mentioned suggests that managers are inclined to think that new technology (CAT systems) will boost productivity automatically. Pava argues persuasively that deficient management and poor organization will never be corrected by tools or gadgets. New learning by reporters and by managers is *central* to developing change in responsibility and to creating new patterns of work coordination called into being by new technology. Seeing the reporting function in a new way requires a vision and a method to make that vision come alive. Pava's work embodies an older managerial theory called sociotechnical design. The social system into which new technology is thrust must "evoke and sustain commitment and involvement" (Pava 1983, 21). This leads to successful adoption of new office technology.

The key to avoiding employee carelessness, inattention, and aggravation when new technology is introduced in a reporter firm is to consider what people want on the job. If people have fair compensation, job security, benefits, safety, and due process, what more could they ask for? Pava lists six psychological job criteria that go beyond the typical rewards for work just listed:

1. Some autonomy and discretion.
2. A chance to learn and continue to learn on the job.
3. A variety of activities to get relief from fatigue and boredom.
4. A chance to help and respect others in exchange for their comparable help and respect.
5. An opportunity to make a meaningful contribution on the job.
6. The prospects of a meaningful future. (Pava 1983, 21)

The major thesis of sociotechnical design applied to the office is that "sociotechnical design explicitly addresses both the technical and social subsystems and their interrelations" (Pava 1983, 24). An organizational theory called organization development, or "OD," focuses on the people, not the technology. That is not enough. The reverse is classical bureaucracy applied to the office and factory which results in a nineteenth-century work design that emphasizes five principles of job design seen through the eyes of production engineers, engineering managers, systems analysts, and data processing managers:

1. Identify maximum operation cycles per unit of time.
2. Use machine resources most efficiently.
3. Make each job as simple as possible.
4. Reduce manpower by substituting machines.
5. Make certain that managers get better information to manage the function.

As Pava notes: "Executives, managers and supervisors tend tacitly to take a similar position, and so design proposals for advanced office information systems are often based upon outmoded concepts" (Pava 1983, 34). In contrast, the sociotechnical design does not elevate the needs of tools over the needs of people at work. Both are important in what Pava calls a "best match." This approach toward management makes a lot of sense.

The position taken from the beginning of this book is that reporting is primarily a human service with a long history of association with a variety of tools. The reporter profession struggled for decades learning to use stenotype reporting equipment. That technology is finally the dominant mode of reporting, but those who prefer Gregg or Pitman shorthand continue to report. Both reporter types struggled with a variety of transcription systems. Now the stenotype machine has become the input device with transcription in CAT flowing from it. Pen writers are now at a more distinct disadvantage to reporters who can use CAT systems and stenotype. The latter can transcribe at high-speed computer rates and use spin-off technology available to them. The waves of technological change have not made prior reporting systems obsolete, but only more inefficient. Over decades of change the bulk of the reporters shift to newer or different technologies.

Never before has there been such attention to a "best match" of the technical and social subsystems of an organization as that provided by Pava's concept of sound organizational strategy toward new technology. It is time that management strategy be considered and that total organizational needs be taken into account in adopting new technology.

If reporters who manage are willing to accept the premise that there is some "best match" of technical and social subsystems, then it is easy to see that the methods of analysis described fully in Pava's book are going to help those managers. Pava distinguishes routine from nonroutine office work and develops procedures for analysis to explore what direction the firm should take in achieving a "best match" of systems. Those interested in Pava's perspective would do well to pursue his approach (Pava 1983).

Other management perspectives should be kept in mind. Although Pava sees his sociotechnical design approach as a form of contingency theory, and uses systems logic, he rejects the classical bureaucratic approach to job design, and may miss some of the human relations aspects. Yet he wants psychological job satisfaction criteria to be used in system design. One reaction to his work is that it is too complex to work in the real world of managing. It is complex, but according to Eric Trist, one of the originators of sociotechnical design, the technological imperative continues to be followed—bad jobs continue to be designed for people by managers and engineers (Pava 1983, 174).

Reporters who manage reporter firms keep one central sociotechnical design idea in mind when they say that reporters should report and others should free them so that they can report. This idea suggests that scopists, editors, or central persons who help reporters, do relieve them of the tasks of note-reading, typing, proofreading, correcting, running, binding, and delivery. With the growing exactness and demanding nature of shorthand reporting using CAT systems, the precision of the reporter should be devoted to that most critical of tasks, that of taking the record. The absolute clarity of input should be the primary concern, with specialization of others flowing from this job design logic. The managers of reporter firms can take on the personnel, financial, marketing and technology-scanning aspects themselves, in order to free the reporter to focus on the note-taking and continuing education parts of reporting. In this manner of conscious job design, enhancing the professional quality of the reporting work is a worthy goal of managing.

TYPES OF TECHNOLOGY

The state of technology serving the reporting profession deserves brief description. In Chapter 1 a general history of the development of the stenotype machine was outlined along with the history of CAT systems for transcription in the last 15 years.

From 1980 to 1985, the growth of CAT and other technology can be measured in a simple way. In 1980 there was little at the NSRA national meeting in Atlanta: "At my first NSRA convention—Atlanta in 1980—the show itself was small and there was a limited presence by computers" (J. Wilson 1984). By 1984 in Las Vegas, there were minicomputers, microcomputers, computerized billing systems, word processing systems, and data-based systems. By 1985, ten CAT vendors displayed their products, and all of them had something new to add to the growing repertoire of products for the computerized court reporter (Schleich 1985). The reviews by Wilson and Schleich are so detailed there is no reason to summarize them except to point to them for those who want more current research information.

A wide range of electronic typewriters and word processors are available to reporters who use manual systems of written notes and dictation systems. Optical scanning of reporter notes is available. Data-based systems for accounting, management information, and other purposes are available. Laser printers, fiber optics, and microform storage are examples of current technology. Complex internal office communication systems, copier systems, and office design firms all open up the concept of office technology far beyond the CAT technology which is at the heart of the most advanced systems. Two other forms of technology, audio tape recording and video systems for video depositions, are available in a wide range of product lines for reporters. The innovative nature of these products and the tendency of the competitive firms to add new products suggest that reporters will be in the mainstream of office innovation in the foreseeable future.

ADOPTING NEW TECHNOLOGY

By now the managing reporter can see that reporters have experienced a major traumatic technological shock from 1980 to 1987. Based upon his national travels as president of NSRA in 1985 Runfola described the shock this way:

> "CAT is the state of the art in our field; not conceptual, not experimental. I expect by the end of my term in office that more than 50 percent of the reporters in the country will be using CAT. (Runfola 1986, 7)

One would expect to see adoption or conversion problems with all of this change going on simultaneously across the nation. In this change process what do reporters experience that managers should note? Some insights are gained by a quick review of published experiences of reporters.

Training

The first few days on a computer system are difficult. Kay Howell offers vivid explanations of a training session troubled by the exactness of "powering up" and "powering down" (Howell 1985). The training sessions are specifically designed by equipment manufacturers to educate users, form user groups, build product loyalty, and provide hot-line systems so that users may quickly receive help. Sometimes manufacturers will store alternate dictionaries built by reporters on CAT systems to safeguard them from fire and other hazards. The relationships are extensive in the CAT field, but eventually reporters are on their own except for sessions with other users, colleagues, and *NSR* articles. The following *NSR* articles are specifically designed for the early conversion or adoption period and for background on the process of change (Nelson 1984a and 1984b; Jorpeland 1984 and 1985; Dunn 1984; Runfola 1984; Wilson 1984a and 1984c; Cramer 1984; Rogner 1984a, 1984b, and 1985b; Sanchez 1984a; Granger 1984; Singer 1984; Drill 1985; Howell 1986; Praino 1986). This broad range of experience reinforces the need for ample training and for enhanced user communication networks. Managers must be aware of these needs of reporters, especially during conversions.

Dictionary Conversions

Another aspect of conversions which is likely to become more significant in the future is related to the conversion of reporter CAT dictionaries from one CAT system to another. Some CAT vendors cease doing business and leave users with dictionaries of 20,000 to 50,000 words or more locked in a dying or dead system. While there is no common format among manufacturers, there is widespread recognition that dictionaries should be formatted to allow for inexpensive, quick, and easy conversion (Schleich 1986).

Transcript Production—Text Processors

The effort to reduce transcript delay led to guidelines for reporter productivity in 1983 (Nelson 1983). This major effort by an NSRA Production Guidelines Task Force is the latest word on guidelines. Of course, CAT systems are directly responsible for easing the burden of transcript preparation, and they will assist in the future by reducing delay to zero. An interesting outgrowth of CAT systems development is the development of specialists, called scopists, or text processors, who took the place of a note-reader in the older configuration of stenotype reporter. The description, text processor, is a neutral-sounding description of a reporter's assistant (Hunt 1986). Five years ago there was no such job as text processing, according to Kevin Hunt. The new position requires work in transcript production, scheduling, computer maintenance, and archival-dictionary maintenance. The CAT experiments in Florida courts have used scopists or text processors to great advantage. This specialization shows how an interest in quality transcripts can lead to new positions in the reporting field.

MANAGEMENT GUIDELINES

Suppose a reporter wanted to buy a CAT system. The Committee on Computer-Aided Transcription of NSRA prepared a series of questions to ask yourself as a reporter, and a series of questions for vendors of CAT systems (NSRA 1985). This guide was almost paralled in Merilyn Sanchez's work on CAT management in the official court reporter field (Sanchez 1984 and 1986). The detail for consideration in the Sanchez work helped to shape the "Management Guidelines for the CAT Pilot Programs" sponsored by the Office of State Courts Administrator for the State of Florida in Tallahassee, Florida in April 1986. The work of Kenneth Palmer, state courts administrator, and Michael Bridenback, his assistant, were vital to the innovative Florida program. These management guidelines included government contracts, court rules, standards, statutes governing court reporters' management, personnel policies, transcript production standards, CAT equipment policies and practices, editorial standards for scopists, and special project guidelines. A growing body of management-related materials is being produced, of which this book will be another contribution.

SPIN-OFFS

One of the joys of technology is people's ability to open their creative powers to recombine and unite aspects of technology or find new applications. The spin-offs from CAT technology are just now being tried and seem to be delightful additions to the scope of reporter activities.

Litigation Support

Law firms have been building litigation support systems for a number of years on an ad hoc basis, especially in very large cases with large numbers of witnesses. Software packages allow attorneys to select data items; identify documents; develop indexes, directories, and word-frequency lists; search for items; and sort, edit, and develop historical tracking of documents (Frost and Dunlap 1983, 287). The libel suit by General William Westmoreland against the Columbia Broadcasting System was a major legal event in 1984. CBS produced 50,000 pages of material, and government agencies turned out about 30,000 pages. Depositions ran for more than 150 days. "The court reporter, using computer-aided transcription (CAT), provided hard copy as well as electronic copy on 9-track tape" (Rust and Meltzer 1986).

The intricate relationship between reporters and litigation support systems is described by Ronald Rust and Curtis Meltzer as follows:

> The interface between computer-aided transcription equipment and personal computers has been greatly enhanced, allowing court reporters to provide their clients an additional service with greater efficiency. . . . As more technological advances are made, the number of applications to the legal community will certainly multiply. (Rust and Meltzer 1986)

CAT and the Rust litigation support firm produced a full text data base consisting of about 10,000 pages of trial transcripts on a personal computer.

One of the reporters who leads in the area of litigation support area is H. Allen Benowitz of Miami, Florida, who summarized key points for reporters. The CAT reporter can deliver transcripts to clients on PC-compatible diskettes. The CAT reporter can copy transcripts onto a nine-track magnetic tape in a format compatible with computers having greater memory that are used either by law firms or by litigation support firms (Benowitz 1986). Other spin-offs include telecommunications, PC-compatible software, and real time translations. The American Bar Association readers are noticing electronic transcript (Johnson 1986).

Courtroom Administrative Data Input—CADI

Under the leadership of past NSRA president Jere With of San Diego, a committee of NSRA developed a system compatible with CAT technology that would enable court reporters to build a separate file of data inputs about the administrative features of courtroom work. For example, the names of the jurors, the time of events in the courtroom, the names of parties, witnesses, attorneys, and judges are usually hand transcribed by courtroom staffs. A court reporter could simply build a small separate electronic file and at the end of each day of trial or any other interval, strip out the administrative information. This prototype system is in the developmental stages but has great potential for recasting data flows inside the courtroom, and among courtrooms and administrative support offices in a court system.

Courtrooms of the Future

The National Shorthand Reporter Association has sponsored the development of "courtrooms of the future" in Detroit, Michigan; Chicago, Illinois; and Phoenix, Arizona. A new "courtroom of the future" is being planned with the National Judicial College in Reno, Nevada. CAT systems are put in place in each of these locations and management systems are developed. The ensuing interest by the judiciary has been great (Rogner 1985c; Wilson 1986a). The state of New Mexico has developed a major CAT project in Albuquerque courts (Wilson 1986b; Galleqos 1986).

Captioning and the Deaf

Since CAT systems may be used in real time (that is, three seconds after speaking, the English word appears on a screen) the development of closed captioned TV for the deaf has taken hold. Reporters are involved in this effort (Block 1984 and 1987). A judge who became deaf has been a recipient of this spin-off of CAT technology (Klink 1984).

Electronic Cottages

The added flexibility of CAT enables the reporters to decentralize their transcription work and telecommunicate it from home or from some other work station. This feature adds new structural complexity to reporter firms by trading reduced costs of rental space for other processing costs of transmitting the data. This feature has great potential for changing the work habits of reporters as does any feature of CAT technology.

Each of the technological spin-offs—litigation support, CADI, courtrooms of the future, captioning, and electronic cottages—is a potential management field that requires the attention of managing reporters.

7

The Future of Management in the Reporting Profession: Strategic Concepts and Strategic Actions in Management

> Future shock ... The shattering stress and disorientation that we induce in individuals by subjecting them to too much change in too short a time.
>
> Alvin Toffler, *Future Shock* 1970.

> The future enters into us, in order to transform itself in us, long before it happens.
>
> Rainer Maria Rilke, *Letter to a Young Poet* (1875–1926)

THE FUTURE, AND INNOVATION AND STABILITY

Grains of truth about the future are scattered widely across the experiences of mankind. CAT technology has introduced plenty of stress of the future shock variety into the lives of some reporters, while other reporters were eagerly waiting for the CAT revolution to happen in 1980 when it became a widespread reality. The future had entered them. The reporter profession follows the usual finding about any group of human beings—some are fast to change while, at the other extreme, some are very reluctant to change.

In one of the best researched books on change and innovation, Everett M. Rogers of Stanford University has developed ideal types of people who adopt innovations of all kinds:

Range of Innovation Adopters

Innovators	*Early Adopters*	*Early Majority*	*Late Majority*	*Laggards*
Venturesome	Respectable	Deliberate	Skeptical	Traditional

These ideal types are used for research purposes to find out something about the socioeconomic characteristics, personality variables, and communication behavior associated with each type of adopter (Rogers 1983, 241–270). Most people fall into the early majority and late majority with much smaller populations at either end of the spectrum. And there are differences in these types. In the reporter field, CAT adopters in 1980 were predominantly in private, free-lance work. In 1990 to 2000, one could expect that those who are skeptical and traditional toward innovation will finally consider adoption of CAT technology, and they may be predominantly in the official reporter group, even though some official reporters were leading the innovation bandwagon for CAT in the mid–1970s.

The change agent aspects of a managing reporter's role are best understood by reviewing what Rogers states about change agents (Rogers 1983, 312–346). One of the most important characteristics of a successful change agent is that he or she has a high degree of homophily, "the degree to which pairs of individuals who interact are similar in certain attributes" (Rogers 1983, 321). Beliefs, education, and social status are examples of these attributes. Homophily also refers to people who resemble each other in their occupations and education, who talk the same language. These persons have a persuasive power with one another that affects the flow of communication (Rogers 1983, 274). And the communication is strong enough to persuade a late adopter finally to give something a try. Education distinguishes one extreme from the other, but in the reporter profession there is greater comparability of education, so that it may have less influence among reporters.

There is a fascinating example of resistance to change by reporters and judges. Some in the federal courts are still trying to encourage the adoption of audio recording, but after years of effort there has been no overwhelming rush to embrace audio recording technology (Meacham 1986). By the end of 1985, there were only 31 active and senior federal judges involved with audio technology. Only 49 of the hundreds of bankruptcy judges requested installations. Something is very unworkable in the federal approach to producing this change. In fact, judges and reporters in federal courts could be considered an unequivocal failure in the adoption of audio technology, especially because the technology has been available for nearly three decades and dates back to the 1930s. But has the true energy of the federal bench been behind this adoption of audio technology? Probably not. Have the federal court reporters embraced audio technology? No way. Rather they have fought its introduction just as reporters have since 1934. Who is now for audio technology in the federal courts? The answer lies in the minds of a few judges and some administrators in the federal court system. However, they probably lack homophily with the majority of judges and court reporters in the federal courts. The advocates are simply not accepted as opinion leaders in the federal courts. And the federal courts are finding reporters turning more fully toward CAT. The president of NSRA, Thomas F. Runfola, stated in early 1986:

CAT vendors tell me they are experiencing record sales in the official-reporting market. As an example, more than 35 percent of the federal court reporters in the country are now computerized. (Runfola 1986, 7)

Federal court reporters present both resistance to change and acceptance of change at the same time.

The central fact of life in reporting is that the National Shorthand Reporters Association took a stand on the use of both audio and video systems and these were the positions:

In 1971, the board (of NSRA) adopted the following policy regarding audio equipment:

1. That the National Shorthand Reporters Association is unalterably opposed to the sole use of electrical recording as a replacement for the shorthand reporter.

2. That the use of electrical recording as a matter of reference by a shorthand reporter is a matter for his own determination (National Shorthand Reporters Association 1976, 67)

In January 1972, the NSRA board adopted the following policy with regard to use of videotape:

1. That the National Shorthand Reporters Association is unalterably opposed to the sole use of videotape as a replacement for the shorthand reporter.

2. A shorthand reporter shall not arrange for or participate in a videotape recording of a deposition unless a stenographic record is simultaneously made. (National Shorthand Reporters Association 1976, 67)

A series of steps from 1972 to 1987 led NSRA and reporters across the nation to adopt a position toward all technology. The policy encourages its use when reporters control and manage the process to protect the integrity of the professional process of making the record. Almost 15 year have come and gone, and these NSRA policies still reflect a wise set of choices by a professional group, not only to preserve the economic life of the profession, but to respond to something deeper in the professional psyche. Reporters must have sensed the human service model of reporting and seen that exclusive reliance on these mechanical recording tools would destroy the human side, the professional side, of reporting. Only they could fully understand the significance of such destruction to record integrity. Even more significant, reporters sensed the meaning of the "indifferent pen of the ever-recording reporter" (Louisell and Pirsig 1953, 41). As explained in more detail in Chapter 1 of this book, the value of an independent record serves the trial judges, trial attorneys, parties to litigation, and appellate judges in a way no other record can satisfy the need for independence and integrity. After the Watergate tapes were so easily altered by the office of a United States president, the position of NSRA remains as sound as ever in terms of values protected by a professional approach to reporting. The integrity of a record is protected by a reporting process involving human professionals under a code of ethics. Ironically, two human reporters took the record of the Watergate hearings in Congress.

MANAGEMENT STRATEGY

Reporters already know the meaning of strategy because they have been exercising this concept at the national level in NSRA for nine decades. And the 1986–1987 president of NSRA, Jay E. Suddreth* of Overland Park, Kansas, urges reporters to develop a strategic management style that is based on these ingredients:

1. Set your range of vision higher that it is today.
2. Form a bigger picture of the world than you hold today.
3. Don't stare at the world—scan it.
4. Make yourself visible to others, and make your opinions known.
5. Always have alternative plans.
6. Practice managing your timing, because timing and positioning are the keys to survival.

And Suddreth concluded: "Never forget that higher shorthand speeds and better quality shorthand writing are essential secrets to our continuing share of the marketplace" (Suddreth 1986, 9).

Management Strategy
Jay E. Suddreth

1. SET YOUR RANGE OF VISION HIGHER THAN IT IS TODAY.

We have all heard about goal setting—short, medium and long-range goals. And as trite as it may sound, the accomplishments we make in the field of court reporting have everything to do with how good our range of vision is as it relates to setting appropriate goals.

As court reporting students, our goal is to complete school, pass the requisite exams, and start working. Unfortunately, once this short-range

*Jay Suddreth expanded from an NSR editorial comment on each of these points for this book; thus the following material is an original contribution by him.

goal has been accomplished by many reporting students, their range of vision beyond this exceptional accomplishment starts to get blurry and out of focus. It then becomes, for many, a humdrum existence of going to work and making money. For the masses, goal setting ceases upon graduation from reporting school.

The National Shorthand Reporters Association offers many vehicles for reporters to enlarge their vision beyond their own backyards. A few would include serving on committees, holding office on the board of directors, attending seminars and conventions, excelling in speed examinations and speed contests, and offering creative input to making court reporting the best possible profession.

All too often we become stuck in the status quo, which results in apathy, a desire to be comfortable, and eventual vulnerability to the various and sundry electronic recorders on the market that claim superiority over traditional reporting methods.

Giving something back to the profession that has been so good to all of us will break the apathy chain and set us free.

2. FORM A BIGGER PICTURE OF THE WORLD THAN YOU HOLD TODAY

Advanced technology and communications have literally made us a part of a global village; yet, many of us neither see nor move beyond the local community in which we live.

We often comment that what happens in South Africa and Nicaragua has no bearing on our lives and jobs as court reporters. What the Russians and Libyans are doing is of no consequence to us unless they are knocking on our doors.

This view is extremely limited. Third World countries, superpowers, and foreign allies and their impact on our lives as reporters are far more relevant that many of us remotely suspect. Everything happens for a purpose, and every event has an impact, however remote. A close examination of world events and geopolitical shenanigans can help give us greater perspective on how to change and alter decisions that we make in our very own hometown in terms of foreign travel, investment decisions, and job direction.

How can busy reporters form a bigger picture of the world and gain greater understanding of global events? One quick and easy method is to read the front page of the *Wall Street Journal* each day. Every major worldwide event that has occurred in the past 24 hours is digested here for quick reading.

If you have additional time, there are many other periodicals available. Each day over 6,000 new books arrive at the book stores of America. Each of us lives within a few miles of a public library, that forgotten bastion of learning. The point is, we have access to all the information we need if we will but take the time to digest it. And having done so, we will gain greater understanding of world civilizations, of ethnic and racial differences, of global economies and their interaction with multinational banks and of the eventual impact on each and every one of us mere mortals.

3. DON'T STARE AT THE WORLD—SCAN IT

It is easy, after years of conditioning, to fall into a rut of working, proofreading, getting the job out, and not moving beyond this vicious circle. In some instances, we literally become zombies in the profession we love so much. Because we drift (sometimes on purpose) into this workaholic environment so easily, we then have less time for other outside activities. We literally begin to stare at the world with no time to move on and take in all the panoply of activities going on around us. As a result, we miss out on a lot of things in which we could participate.

It has also been said that knowledge is doubling about every four to six years. If this is true, we do not have time to stare or we will certainly fall behind. We have to adopt a "scan" style for the management of people and activities or we are left in the dust. More critical and sensitive decisions can sometimes benefit from a "stare" style of management, but too often we miss the point by concentrating (staring) too heavily on one issue.

Scanning will enable us to do more in faster ways and to stay current. For those who prefer the old-fashioned way of doing things, staring will always be in vogue. This group could include reporters reluctant to go on computer because of fear or age or undisclosed reasons. If they would but take time to scan the possibilities of the big picture, many of these excuses would evaporate into thin air.

4. MAKE YOURSELF VISIBLE TO OTHERS, AND MAKE YOUR OPINIONS KNOWN

During my year as president of the National Shorthand Reporters Association, I received hundreds of calls from reporters all across the country. Many were plaintive pleas for help to save them from electronic recording. Others were positive suggestions on how I could do my job better. Certainly these people were making their opinions known by calling me on the phone. Many could have derived even better results if they had been more visible at seminars, conventions, or state and national association meetings. Connecting a voice with a face, most of the time, is a great asset in making decisions that affect the lives and jobs of many people.

Each year when the NSRA nominating committee meets to consider interested candidates for positions on the NSRA Board of Directors, the list of names submitted is short and many times inadequate. The memberships' reluctance to make the time commitment and financial sacrifices each year the committee meets is clearly evident. Without this sacrifice and commitment, the future leadership and strength of NSRA becomes severely limited, and the profession as a whole will suffer.

Those members who are qualified and interested in making the necessary concessions in their personal lives to save their association are to be commended. Unfortunately, they seem to be far and few between.

Increased visibility before your peers, assuming you meet the other qualifications, is a sure prescription for being given the opportunity to serve at the state and national level.

5. ALWAYS HAVE ALTERNATIVE PLANS

Contingency planning is as essential for court reporters as it is for a surgeon or a member of Congress. The day we complete court reporting school and commence court reporting for fun and profit is the day that "Plan B" should go into effect. Without being extremely negative, we can play the "what if" game to help develop the appropriate "Plan B." What if I accidentally cut my finger off sawing wood, wacking a head of cabbage, or mowing the grass? What if I developed a serious hearing loss and could no longer report? What if I developed a serious disease and could no longer make a living? What if I had a serious illness and had a lengthy and expensive hospital stay with no insurance in force? And no disability income to pay my bills? What if, through the magic of voice-to-print, court reporters were no longer needed as they are today?

These are all very sobering questions, but certainly questions that need answers—RIGHT NOW. Contingency planning is absolutely critical to assure peace of mind, financial stability, and security in court reporting as well as in any other profession where critical skills are required.

"Plan B" can be as simple as attending your local community college and taking night classes leading to a degree in another area of interest. It can be attending the External Degree Program offered by the National Shorthand Reporters Association in conjunction with the University of Alabama. It can be taking steps to become proficient in a hobby or avocation that could eventually produce a livable income in an emergency. It can even be a plan to save a portion (at least 10%) of your income systematically to give you increased financial security.

A court reporter who is operating without a "Plan B" or effective contingency plan for the future is most certainly a reporter who (1) has a very short range of vision, (2) is incapable of forming a bigger picture of the consequences that could result from poor planning, (3) is in a trance thinking disaster could never happen to him, and (4) probably cares little about others and does not work as a team member to help the profession or association make things better.

Suddreth suggests: "It's a . . . method that makes the effects of unforeseen events less harmful and more manageable for us" (Suddreth 1986, 9). This logic is bound to require more work, but it should help reporters to survive by adapting where required.

It is easy to see that reporters take strong, reasonable policy stances on a national basis, yet they recognize that professional survival depends on intelligent adaption, not merely giving in to any force in the world around them. Management is intended to fit within a larger framework that reporters have developed over almost a century, while fulfilling their professional destinies. A philosophy of management can emerge from such an array of experiences.

CERTIFIED MANAGING REPORTER PROGRAM

CMR Needs in the Profession

To develop a certified management program, the national leadership of NSRA has spent many years considering management needs and trying to figure out what strategies would work best for reporters. The evolutionary process in developing strategy toward management is understood better by reviewing the thoughts of William Oliver, Jerome E. Miller, and John D. Boverie. During an interview published in the March 1982 issue of *NSR* (NSR, 1982), the following comments were made about management needs of the reporter profession. At the time of this writing it is important to realize that the next presidents, William Oliver (1987–1988) and Jerry Miller, (1988–1989) are both Certified Managing Reporters. Oliver managed in the Detroit, Michigan, Circuit Court and Miller manages in the Chicago, Illinois, Circuit Court, both major state trial courts of general jurisdiction. These court systems are among the largest in the nation.

In 1982, John Boverie began articulating the need for managing reporters:

> I have almost 29 years of reporting in the courts, beginning back in 1952. The tradition of one judge/one reporter has been the norm. And yet in the courts today I see things occurring that didn't occur two or three decades ago. I see the imposition of duties with which the reporter had no concern when I first started reporting.
>
> Consequently, I see a need today in many courts all over the country for someone with guts enough to stand up and face certain judges eye to eye and say, "Judge, you are killing your reporter. You're going to have to ease up."
>
> About three years ago I conducted a survey in Colorado of certain reporting practices. I found that in one county when their judges were gone, and there was no reporting to be done, reporters were being ordered into the court clerk's office to do microfilming. It didn't matter how much transcript load these reporters had: they were simply told to sit down and answer the phone, microfilm files, or whatever.
>
> In another county I found that the reporter was being ordered by her judge to prepare free transcripts, which were then filed and became the appeal transcripts.

She did not get paid for transcribing, most of which she had to do after hours—she not only had to turn them out for free but sometimes on an expedited basis.

I found one reporter who had had no vacation for three years. Why not? Because her judge, who loved to sit on the bench, took no vacations. No vacation for three years, and no prospect for one. The judge was wearing out his reporter.

In one western Colorado city a reporter was doing all the clerk's work—not only reporting but setting up the docket, getting the files, doing the judge's correspondence. She had two jobs, though hired for only one.

I suspect if a similar survey were done of all courts in the United States, it would unearth many similar findings. We have reporters who are being loaded down with an appeal rate or a transcript load without any chance of really getting caught up. They work night and day. Some find notereaders, but that doesn't solve all their problems. These reporters don't have much of a life except work—their spouses see them maybe on Sundays.

Problems do exist in the courts for court reporters. Who will be the reporters' voice? Who is going to run interference for them when things go wrong? Their state associations are supposed to be the reporter's first line of defense, but these days state associations are so busy dealing with legislative and other matters that they rarely get down to working out one-on-one problems that occur in court.

In September 1979, Sandra W. McFate, then NSRA president, appointed the Certified Managing Reporter Task Force. We, as members of this task force, feel that there is an answer to the problem of who will speak for the reporter. And the answer lies in the development and training of a corps of managing reporters.

Why We Need Managing Reporters. The first question that has to be answered, before we go further, is why? Why have a program? Why have court reporters do the managing?

And the first answer as to why we should have court reporters managing reporting services in the big courts is that reporters have the background to understand: to understand work problems, understand the flow of work, understand how to move people in order to move the work and equalize the transcript work load.

The second reason for having a reporter managing reporters is simply that the reporter is more concerned with both the professional and the mechanical aspects than is any judge, clerk, or court administrator. The judge wants the job filled and the job done but doesn't want to worry about the how, or the problems that occur. The clerk wants the transcripts filed so they can move on out to the appellate court. The court administrator is concerned with budgets, with numbers, but not necessarily with the feelings of the people involved. The court reporter is concerned, because he has been there, he understands the problems. The reporter is better able to act as a problem-solving clearinghouse than is the judge, the clerk, the secretary, or the court administrator.

Lastly, court reporters are intelligent people. They have the skills, the brains, and the ability to manage.

We know that around the country there do exist today many chief reporters, or senior reporters or administrative reporters, who are doing some or all of the job of managing court reporting services. No two of them are alike. We have tyrants among court reporters; we also have pussycats that anybody can push over.

How do we bring some order out of the chaos that is the management of reporting services? First, once the Board of Directors has approved the program, we need to have education, since it's the view of the task force that there can be no certification without education. It can't happen overnight. My best guess is that if we can get started on this reasonably soon, it will probably be around 1984 or 1985 before we really start certifying people as managing reporters.

The education needs to start off with the fundamentals of how to manage, how to supervise, how to lead—and to continue to work on management skills right up to personnel management, scheduling, and on into accounting and the budgeting process. We also need to teach those tyrants how to be democratic; we need to train the pussycats how to snarl when necessary. We need to educate with a view to certification.

In the long run we would hope to arrive at the point where we have people who are in uniform, who are neither tyrants or pussycats, who can go to a judge and ask for—and get—certain things and yet be able to go to reporters and get the optimum amount of work out without overtaxing anyone.

Part of the certification and education program will require a heavy emphasis on role-playing. We must not create more tyrants, reporters whipping other reporters just to get the job done. To succeed, the managing reporter has to do certain things and refrain from doing certain other things, and that becomes education. (NSR 1982)

Lions or Pussycats

In 1982 Oliver assessed the need for managing reporters in the following manner:

It's exciting for me to be here: First, because of the program we're trying to establish, and second, because it would be a pleasure to see other people in the same position I'm in. I started my position as managing court reporter about four years ago.

One point I want to make is that we must stand up for what we think is right. It's also important that we demonstrate we are more skillful in managing ourselves than anyone else can be. We want to be controlled by ourselves. Why? Because we are knowledgeable people: we know what needs to be done.

First we must define what a managing court reporter is. That's rather difficult. We can compare it somewhat with an administrator on any type of job, but not all colleges and universities around the country agree on what an administrative job should be.

We do know, however, that the person who is a managing reporter or administrator must assume different functions from what the reporter now does. I'm a skilled reporter, and I work basically by myself. I may have a transcriber that I work with, or a computer, but fundamentally I'm Bill Oliver working with Bill Oliver. It's important to be able to leave our basic skills and go into the next area. We're like going from a bachelor's to a master's degree. We're going to have to learn to function differently.

As John Boverie suggests, we're also going to have to decide whether to be lions or pussycats. Will we be strong enough to defend the reporters when the need arises? Will we be strong enough to keep the reporters in line when they're in the wrong?

We want to protect our profession and its members from all calamities. We want the fortune to be ours rather than to have misfortune come upon us. We hear a lot these days about technology and how it's affecting us. Unfortunately, many of us look at it negatively instead of positively. A great deal of technology has come to us, as reporters, that we can use to our benefit. Maybe it will take managing reporters to help us develop it collectively. We have advanced more in the area of technology than have the recording devices. And I know what I'm speaking of, since I worked under a federal grant to make a comparison study of various types of technology.

In helping us develop this program, you as members of NSRA have to be honest with us and honest with yourselves in what we're trying to develop and what all of us really want. Rest assured that one of these days there will be somebody governing the court reporter, whether official or free-lance. Do we want to be that somebody, or do we want it to be done by people outside the realm of reporting?

What is management? It's a skill that deals with achievement. In developing the Certified Managing Reporter, we want to develop in that individual an additional skill to help achieve that goal.

Management skill is not an innate characteristic. You can be potentially a fantastic leader, but unless you develop your abilities along that line it means nothing.

I think it's important that we have skilled reporters to take these management positions. In our own courts, had someone come in under our grant who didn't understand all the idiosyncrasies of reporting, the court would be controlling the CAT system. We felt it was important that the reporters control it, and our grant so states.

Some of the things I myself am involved in concern the development of the reporting budget and the per-diem reporters: how to get and keep skilled reporters on a per-diem basis. And it's extremely important for me to be a PR person, to be able to approach lawyers and judges. Why? Because they really don't know what we do. They know that we sit there and do this and that; they order a transcript and they pay us great sums of money; some of them mistakenly think we're getting rich. But they don't know what happens.

I'm with the circuit court, but I've made it a point, after three years, to know all the judges involved with the appellate court. Because of one program I've instituted, and the communication I have with my people, through monthly reports of pending transcript I know just what each reporter's situation is. I've literally been able to keep reporters from being incarcerated, because I could go in with these sheets and say, "Jane Doe has had x number of pages, she has produced x number of pages so far this month, she has x number of orders."

So what? "Do you realize," we say to the judges, "that it takes this amount of time to produce this much transcript for the number of hours in court?" They didn't know that. I think it's important for us to establish communication so that we can make our situation understood. And again keep in mind that if we don't do it, someone else will (NSRA 82)."

Miller's Law—Reporters Can Manage

Miller of the Chicago Circuit Court, is deputy administrator of one of the largest reporter groups in trial courts in the nation. In 1982 Miller assessed the need for CMR positions this way:

One thing that should be clarified and emphasized here, is that neither NSRA nor this task force is advocating or insisting that there be managing reporters in every jurisdiction of the country. Rural jurisdictions that have a one-on-one situation with judges and reporters will probably stay that way. But if you look at the overall reporting picture in the large metropolitan areas, you see a tendency to adopt a "pool-type" operation.

These pools will need supervision. What NSRA and this task force are trying to accomplish is to see that court reporters aren't overlooked when it comes to selecting supervisors or managers. Reporters should have the same opportunity to fill these positions as anyone from any other management field. And this program is to assist them to obtain the expertise to qualify as capable managers.

I would say that the reporting profession and the reporters themselves are capable of handling the managing reporter concept and should be given the opportunity. Managers should not have to come from outside our ranks. We can train ourselves—and I'm sure there are now many reporters more than qualified to take on the task of managing reporter. I hope this program will help them achieve this goal, should they aspire to it (NSR 1982)."

Jerry Miller reflected further on the idea of selecting reporters to fill management positions by writing another article:

Many court administrators will tell you that reporters can't manage themselves because they lack the objectivity needed for good management decisions. But we in the profession feel just the opposite.

One of the problems, though, in managing ourselves and setting up the new self-management approach is dealing with the effects of the widely publicized "management revolution" that this country experienced in the late '60s and early '70s. The management concepts of that era categorized a manager into a variety of styles: "autocrat," "hardliner," "bottom-liner," "country-clubber," "democrat," and on and on.

Managers who attended seminars or read the latest bible on management were usually able to identify their style without much problem—and then, with this renewed confidence of having a "recognized" style, proceeded to apply it to their workplace without considering other changes that had taken place.

Most managers followed a strictly regimented rules-and-regulations style, overlooking societal changes and changes in attitude in the working world.

One of the main topics in management discussions relating to theories of management dealt with the need of the modern manager to be "democratic" in his relationship with his subordinates ("subordinate" also had connotations that weren't quite acceptable to the new thinking) and still maintain a sense of authority and control in those areas in which he was responsible.

Before the '50s and '60s, management style was not considered that important an issue. It was always assumed that successful managers possessed the intelligence, drive, and experience to make quick, dependable decisions and to inspire their subordinates to achieve work-related goals.

The new thinking that evolved from the social sciences stressed group interaction, focusing on the workers in the group and not just the leader. Seminars were designed and conducted to give people experience in this new concept. Many of the participants thought this style of management was very "democratic"; they returned to their organizations wanting to put these new ideas into effect.

The more enthusiastic alumni of these sessions tended to label management as either democratic or authoritarian, depending on the amount of worker participation involved in decision-making. This research and training resulted in the questioning of the stereotype of an effective manager. As a result, the modern manager found himself uneasy, torn between being an "authoritative" or "permissive" leader.

What Is Your Style? Many supervising or managing reporters, I imagine, find themselves in this dilemma. This is especially true because of the changes taking place in our profession through technology, reduction in budgets and work force, federal and state statute changes, and movements in labor organizations that challenge the right of managers to make decisions without considering the effect on people within and outside the organization. Then there is the national concern for quality of work life and its relationship to workers' production, participation, and satisfaction in their working environment.

Keeping in mind these external forces that affect the management style, here are some theories of developing a more "democratic" approach.

The "autocratic" manager in his normal problem-solving would identify the problem, consider alternative solutions, select one of them, and submit this decision to his subordinates to carry out. He might or might not give consideration to their thought in his decision; in any event, he would afford them no chance to take part in the decision-making process.

A beginning of the "democratic" process would be to "sell" his decision rather than simply announcing it. In so doing, he recognizes that there may be some resistance; this he will seek to reduce by pointing out some of the benefits to be gained from this solution.

Another alternative would be to invite questions from the group, thus allowing exploration and understanding of the effects of his decision.

A step further would be to make a tentative decision, first thinking the problem through, arriving at a decision, and then suggesting an open, frank discussion on the solution and his tentative decision. The manager is now saying, let me hear what you have to say, but I'll still have the final word.

What is taking place here is that the manager gradually capitalizes on the group's experience and understanding from actual on-the-job involvement. From this stage he can go full circle by asking them to identify the problem and suggest solutions, which he may then accept. He may also participate in this group decision-making process, while trying to exercise no more authority than the other members of the group.

The group participation allowed by the manager may not reflect a true picture of this "democratic" managerial attitude. If he shares only the minor decisions, reserving the major ones for himself, this may cause resentment from the group and defeat his good intentions.

I have learned from experience in managing reporters that in general one should not overmanage—and that this works to everyone's advantage.

Reporters Have Good Management Potential. Reporters who have worked in the various free-lance offices and as officials have been exposed to many and varied managerial styles and from this exposure would themselves be capable of handling management responsibilities. A good guess would be that most of these styles developed through work-related experience and good old common sense.

The future of the managing reporter should be one of great challenge, imagination, and style-setting. Gary Cramer's article in the June 1982 *NSR* gives examples of reporter management in the reporting field of the future. Introduction of any new technology into older systems, allowing for resistance from those who feel it won't work or comes much too soon, will really test the mettle of the manager thrust into such situations.

As we look at other segments of industry in today's economy and read some of the horror stories of businesses faltering and going "belly-up," there is always the exception of the imaginative and flexible manager whose innovative style has helped him and his business to survive.

The reporting profession will not lack survivors willing to accept the challenges of modern technology, adapting to those techniques that are adaptable to our work, demonstrating the impracticality of those that aren't. We have the tools to manage our own destinies. I am confident that many innovative management styles will develop in our profession.

An article that I recently read may just hold the secret to developing a successful managerial style. It told of an interview with Professor C. Northcote Parkinson, promulgator of Parkinson's First Law ("Work expands to fill the time available") and a number of equally trenchant "laws." The professor told of a certain Minister during the years immediately following World War II. Young civil servants would bustle into his office waving documents, emphasizing the high priority of this and the top secrecy of that. He would listen patiently and tell each young man to leave his paper on the desk. Then as the youngster reached the door, he would call out:

> "Oh, one thing, Mr. Davenart."
> "Sir?"
> "Remember Rule Six."
> "Yes, sir, of course."

Then the young man would reach the door and turn back, having had another thought:

> "Excuse me, sir, what is Rule Six?"
> "Rule Six is as follows: Don't take yourself too seriously."
> "Thank you, sir, I'll remember that."

Once more the young man would be at the door with his hand on the doorknob and would turn again as a new idea struck him.

> "But, sir," he would ask, "what are the other rules?"
> "Young man," would come the reply, "there are no other rules."

I think I'll suggest this as the motto for the CMR (Certified Managing Reporter) candidates. (Miller 1983)

A COURT ADMINISTRATOR'S PERSPECTIVE

Court reporters work closely with court administrators in the trial courts of the nation. In Sarasota, Florida, the court administrator, John G. Byers, is both a former court reporter and now an administrator of courts. This position gives him a special perspective on the managing reporter programs. Byers has been president of the National Association of Trial Court Administrators and has worked with NSRA in development of reporter production guidelines and the CADI and CMR programs. Byers has a CAT experiment in his courts. His views follow.

Court Administrator Byers observes:

Managing court reporters is an extremely complicated task that should only be attempted by one who understands the complexities of the reporter profession. One who assumes that the reporter merely creates on stenotype paper and electronic cassette the words spoken at a trial or hearing, and later reduces it to the printed word, is guaranteed to fail in managing reporters.

The manager needs to be aware of reporter salaries, benefits, costs for reporting materials, furniture, supplies, etc. Other areas of concern are monitoring the transcript delivery time extension requests from the appellate court. This can only be accomplished successfully if management is aware of the designation dates and monitors the production schedule on a daily or weekly basis.

Standards and policies should be uniform throughout a judicial circuit and, under ideal circumstances, should be utilized on a statewide basis under the supervision of the state's highest appellate court. These standards should include, but not be limited to, recording standards, transcription standards and guidelines, payment information for transcripts, production time standards, extension guidelines, administrative controls, salary and benefits for reporter and clerical employees, as well as general housekeeping rules for employees. These should be in written form and available to all employees as well as managers. Everyone should know the rules and work under the same standards. Attorneys should also be given copies of the standards and guidelines so they can be aware of what is expected of them in the appellate process; i.e. filing times for designations, forms for ordering transcripts, and payment for completed transcripts. Formal procedures and regulated policies can and will reduce delay in the appellate process. It is the responsibility of the managing assistant or managing reporter to make sure everyone adheres to the standards and policies once they are established.

Sanctions must be a part of the process. Persons not performing their work in the specified time and manner must be held accountable for their noncompliance. The sanctions *must be formalized* and made a part of the standards and policy manual. To do less will surely create delay in the appellate process, as well as cause morale problems among reporters and clerical assistants.

Managers must be aware of policies or rules requiring preferential treatment for certain types of transcripts. Do criminal appeal cases come before civil cases? Only by constant monitoring of transcript requests can the manager assign reporters to a court, while allowing others to work on transcript preparation and in this process assuring that the workload is properly distributed.

Having the proper resources available for reporters to do their jobs is the responsibility of the Court Administrator. He or she must be aware of the production expenses on a monthly basis. This will enable the administrator to prepare a proper budget for the reporting function. Managers must have facts and figures available during the budget preparation work sessions. Management, in order to explain to state or local fiscal officers, has a duty to the reporters to be able to explain why salaries and benefits should be increased, why transcript rates are expensive, and why new technology will assist in the judicial process. Only by being thoroughly familiar with the reporting process and the production requirements can a manager adequately defend budget requests made at the local or state level.

Proper management of reporters must include informing trial judges of special situations such as daily copy requests, and why it may be necessary to rotate reporters in and out of court. Judges must be made aware of the fact that performance levels diminish after several hours of reporting. It is management's responsibility to provide good working conditions for reporters. Again, I can not put enough emphasis on the fact that a manager *must* know all the stages of the reporting process in order to properly manage and supervise court reporter services

PAINFUL REVISIONISM OR RELIABLE PROFESSIONALISM?

The philosophy of management strategy that comes from decades of personal experiences in a reporter firm and from experiences in NSRA is developed next by Ervin G. Gross, a free-lance reporter from Minneapolis, Minnesota. He was president of NSRA in 1981 and it was during his term that the CMR program began to be formulated. The Certified Managing Reporter (CMR) program has a complex background and rationale that Gross knows in detail. The following material was prepared by Gross especially for this book.

Management. Professionalism. These two words very simply sum up the key elements that are so necessary to maintain a strong and independent judiciary.

It was Chief Justice Warren E. Burger who, in the early 1970s, provided the impetus for management and professionalism in the courts. As a result, two major organizations, the Institute for Court Management and the National Center for State Courts, were formed to carry out the development of this theme. With the assistance of federal LEAA funds these organizations have researched and experimented with a variety of topics and theories, and have set in motion a host of changes designed to improve the administration of justice—and hopefully improve public confidence in the system. How well have they done?

As is the case with all newly created organizations which are given mandates to develop new procedures, there follows an inevitable period of revisionism and subsequent soul searching. For example, the educational system certainly found this to be true. The experimental theories of teaching in the public schools were prevalent in the 1960s and 1970s with emphasis on total freedom of expression and a search for "Who am I?" The painful revisionism was found wanting and required serious reexamination when it became clear that Johnny and Mary could not spell, read, write, or do basic arithmetic. There was a tremendous price paid in this country in the form of lost productivity because of an inability to communicate. As a result, the three R's became important in the analysis of that experiment, and a period of revisionism followed.

A similar example is Chief Justice Burger's speech entitled "American Hostages to Crime," in which he questioned the prevailing wisdom of the past 20 years in dealing with technicalities of defendants in the criminal justice system at the expense of the public. Again the lesson is clear. When embarking on a new theoretical course, there must be great care to build on the proven reliability of what has existed in the past. Progressive change to improve efficiency must be thoughtfully undertaken so as not to throw out the baby with the bathwater. A counterproductive course that ignores lessons of the past eventually creates more problems than it solves.

One vital aspect of the court system that has undergone considerable scrutiny is court reporting. A reliable reporting network is obviously a key factor in maintaining public confidence in a strong and efficient judiciary. It must provide a reliable, accurate, and timely record of the proceedings for appeal purposes.

Because of Chief Justice Burger's mandate to examine every avenue of the judiciary in an effort to speed up the system of justice, court administrators have spent a great amount of time analyzing court reporting. The National Center for State Courts has also devoted a considerable amount of time and money to the same subject. As a result, in recent years there has been substantial focus on traditional reporting practices as a cause of court delay. This has been followed by the premise that audio recording may well provide an economical panacea. While there has been no clear documentation that has stood the test of time to that effect, there have been some who support that view. However, an article by Professor Michael H. Graham (Graham 1977) and a study entitled "A Financial Analysis of Electronic Reporting in Alaska" (RPC Report 1978), and others, refute that contention. A typical comment to illustrate the growing sense of revisionism was made recently by a state hearing administrator who nine years ago predicted a very bleak future for court reporting. Now he believes that the present attitude and new practices of reporters who use state of the art technology is providing a litigation support service that makes the future bright for the reporter profession.

The Local Legal Culture

In the National Center for State Courts study on court delay involving 17 metropolitan courts, the basic finding was that delay was not inevitable, and was not determined by the size of the court, the case load of the judge, or the percentage of cases going to trial, but primarily resulted from the desires and attitudes of the people in the system (Church 1978). Thus, a new phrase emerged: "The local legal culture determines the pace of litigation." The authors of the study concluded that *proper management* is the key to solving the problems, and that it is not necessarily techniques that make a court system work, but people and their attitudes. This study would certainly indicate that it has been an oversimplification to make the court reporting system a scapegoat for court delay.

At about the same time, Judge Leonard E. Hoffman of Dallas, Texas, serving as chairman of an ad hoc committee dealt with a study on court reporters and transcription of appellate records. His report suggested that few trial courts and court reporters are involved in the newsworthy situations that have attracted the attention of those interested in attaining a well-regulated judicial system; therefore, there should not be an overreaction on the part of the judiciary or the legislature. He also said that problems do exist and that the situation can be improved without damaging the delicate balance so necessary to our judicial system.

The question legitimately arises: has there been an overreaction on behalf of those charged with analyzing the court reporting system? By threatening reporters with replacement by machines, by electronic recording, albeit primarily in courts of low volume, is there a danger of setting off a counterproductive chain of events that will ultimately affect the public's right to a reliable, accurate, and timely record when the eventual revisionism ensues? By suggesting replacement of reporters with audio recording through attrition of professional reporters, there cannot help but be an interruption in the attraction of competent people to court reporter schools.

On the other side of the coin, there can be no arguing with the premise that court reporting must be effectively managed, and it must have the highest degree of professionalism. There must be realistic production standards and sanction procedures for untimely transcript delivery. However, great care must be taken not to succumb to the temptation of weakening rather than improving a system of reliable reporting by threatening its future with a substandard, nonprofessional audio system operated by judges, clerks, and poorly-trained assistants, that by all standards has its greatest weakness in producing a final transcript in an accurate and timely fashion. How does this square with Chief Justice Burger's reform movement accenting speed and professionalism? In reality, it is a shortsighted, disservice to the judicial branch.

Fostering Productive Relationships

In a report about the Wingspread Conference on Contemporary and Future Issues in the Field of Court Management, the authors stated that initially there was a considerable dichotomy in the relationship between policy making and policy administering, between judges and court administrators:

It is a threatening realization that policy making and policy administering inevitably blend. Judges are threatened when they realize that they are in fact sharing administrative power they had long thought was exclusively theirs. Court administrators are threatened because they might lose their jobs if the realization upsets the judges, or others, such as legislators. (Nejelski 1980)

The report suggests that this original dichotomy is abating, and that this condition has fostered a situation of shared power between judge and administrator. There is a growing acceptance of the idea that a case, once filed, becomes the business of the public and that court personnel, as the public's agents, are responsible for reliably managing the case to disposition.

How Can the CMR Help?

In an effort to assist judges and court administrators who have borne the brunt of management responsibility, the CMR program has a stated purpose of bringing a level of management expertise to the reporting profession that will maximize its productivity, efficiency, and reliability as a protector of the litigant's constitutional right to an accurate and timely record. The CMR, acting as liaison among the administrator, judge, and reporter, can contribute in specialized management areas dealing with staffing, notes archiving, transcript production, budget planning, morale, grievances, discipline, scheduling, and many other areas.

The American Bar Association's Action Commission to Reduce Court Costs and Delay has expressed an interest in ascertaining whether CAT can make a significant contribution in solving the problem of delay in litigation. Many judges, court administrators, attorneys, and court reporters are convinced that CAT can solve that problem.

A 14-month CAT analysis project conducted by the National Center for State Courts, indicated that CAT technology can and does work, but the way in which it is managed in the court environment will determine its efficiency (Delaplain 1981). The report states that benefits that could result from court use of CAT can be grouped under the general headings of cost and time savings, plus intangible benefits that cannot be quantified.

Harnessing Technology Effectively

It is in the management of a CAT program that vast benefits can be realized in case flow management. Records, statistics, and information system management can be vastly improved through proper CAT management by applying database information to the existing court computer system.

Recent dramatic improvements in CAT technology have resulted in widespread acceptance of its use by the reporting profession. The spin-off of sophisticated litigation support now furnished by private reporters to attorneys requires competent management. The "courtrooms of the future" currently in place around the country provide instantaneous translation of testimony that can be viewed on screens and terminals by attorneys and judges. The CMR is trained to administer this array of new services to the courts in an efficient and productive manner.

In 1981, NSRA's Blue Ribbon Task Force interviewed 69 key professional people in 13 states to develop an objective view of present and future shorthand reporting (Gross and Jorpeland 1984). Interviewed were 11 state supreme court justices, 16 trial court judges, eight state court administrators, 13 trial court administrators, 18 trial attorneys, and 3 other professionals connected with the legal system. With regard to the management role of reporters, the consensus of the respondents was that reporters should have a role in the allocation and supervision of day-to-day reporting services including reporter technology, and that management training will help them to effectively aid administrators and judges. As one state supreme court justice commented, reporters' management of reporting services, regardless of the technology being used, is an eminently sensible approach. Donald Cullen, president of the National Association for Court Management, commenting on the CMR program, stated: "First of all, the potential for CMRs would place the responsibility for court reporter services with court reporters. Second, it would provide a basis for managers from two different disciplines—court reporters and court administrators—to communicate on a common ground, namely on a management level" (Gross 1986).

Regis Taylor, an official reporter in Honolulu, Hawaii, who is nearing completion of the CMR program, said:

> Things I'm learning in this program I use every day. Never before have I had the good fortune to encounter such a relevant educational program. Applying these managing techniques to court reporting systems will produce a benefit that in years to come will be compared with the advent of formal training for court administrators. (Taylor and Kennedy 1986)

Lori Kennedy, who owns a free-lance agency in Santa Ana, California, and is a CMR student, said: "The CMR Institute points the way to our future as managers. Through these modules we can establish guidelines that will apply to any management structure, but with a broad-based emphasis on the court reporting community" (Taylor and Kennedy 1986).

First National Symposium

With the tremendous number of sophisticated changes taking place in court reporting it follows that there would be great benefit to the judicial system and the public to have a cooperative force in place which would take advantage of management and professionalism. In 1981, as NSRA president,

I attended the First National Symposium on Court Management in San Diego. The sponsors of the symposium were the Conference of State Court Administrators, the National Association of Court Administrators, the National Association of Trial Court Administrators, the National Conference of Appellate Court Clerks, and the National Council for Judicial Planning. There was considerable emphasis on the partnership role between judges and court administrators, and the importance of sensitivity to each other's position in order to achieve a confident and efficient relationship. I was struck by the parallel between the relationship of judges and administrators, and that of court reporters in their interaction with those two groups. The parallel is that there are special skills and knowledge that each brings to the other, and to the entire judicial system. Such skills and knowledge are a combination of efficiency, productivity, and reliability. The goal of the CMR program is to contribute to that set of relationships through expanded managerial expertise of reporters as part of the judicial team.

This concludes the special contribution of Ervin Gross.

THE DURABLE PROFESSION OF REPORTING

The reporter profession is a solid and durable profession that has been slowly developing into a national force over the last century. At the 75th anniversary of NSRA in 1976, there was a review from the first convention of NSRA (in 1899). New gadgets, like the typewriter, were then being observed and demonstrated and by 1909, in Denver, J. D. Strachan presented a paper on the subject of machine shorthand. This was decades before the widespread use of stenotype equipment in the field. "Although none present foresaw its role in the future, this new system was to revolutionize tbe profession" (NSRA 1976, 48). Professional ethics, along with technology, arose right at the start of NSRA activities.

The durable nature of the reporter profession is further highlighted by Frank O. Nelson (NSRA 1976, 84–86). Nelson wrote about the early history of CAT development and is one who "kept the faith, and continued to preach the gospel of CAT." The early efforts required court reporters to relate to computer types. There were many blind alleys and discouraging tasks; many became disenchanted with CAT in the middle 1960s. Nelson says: "It was concluded by computer personnel at first that court reporters would have to accommodate the machines by changing writing styles and systems. New stenotype systems were developed and advocated. Court reporter resistance grew to new proportions" (NSRA 1976, 85). This sounds exactly like reporters having to accommodate themselves to audio or video approaches. Resistance to audio and video technology also developed. It sounds more than a little reminiscent of the job design approach that Calvin Pava characterized as nineteenth-century industrial engineering job design. People (reporters), must conform to machines—not machines to people.

Since the stenotype machine was ergonomically designed for harmonious linking of the brain and hands, it seems odd, in retrospect, to think that early computer approaches were at first so thoughtlessly rigid. Emery Trist would say, the technological imperative was alive and well in job design for reporters in the early period.

In 1968 and 1969, Frank Nelson and others saw something new emerging. The best way to grasp this critical moment when reporter durability shows up, is when Nelson says:

> In 1968 and 1969 third generation computers began to have their impact upon the CAT program. The realization that the "hardware" could be adopted to meet the needs of shorthand writers drastically changed the approach to the computer "software" development. . . . The magnetic tape cartridge eliminated the need for the court reporter to relinquish original notes to computer people for processing. (NSRA 1976, 85)

Thereafter, the developments quickly fell into place so that the prototype to current CAT systems was, in fact, emerging. The period from 1970 to 1975 was one high point of creativity in CAT development. By 1975 even Nelson could say, "Slowly, CAT is proving to be as feasible as the electric light, television, and jet travel" (NSRA 1976, 86). Nelson recalled his first move, in 1976, to a smaller computer away from the large main frame systems; in 1976 the CAT system actually fit into his office. No more transcontinental data transmission for him.

The legacy that NSRA professional activities leave to this world is one that illustrates the strong, durable, and intelligent nature of the reporter profession. While the NSRA policies directed toward the limits on use of audio and video technology were developed, announced, and modified at the national level, reporters were working hard to bring life to an infant concept of CAT. Reporters showed strength of character, intelligence, and courage by acting with powerful tenacity in both directions. Compared with reporters, I doubt whether any other professional group has been so challenged by events and has challenged others so directly. This baptism of fire has tempered the strength of the profession, and leaves it in a stronger position than ever while closing in upon the year 2000. The reporter profession seems more fit for the future than at any other time in its long history of development.

The United States Census Bureau estimated the United States total population on January 1, 1987, at 242.1 million people, up 15.5 million from the actual count in 1980. This is a 6.4% growth which is unevenly distributed—with very large growth in some states like Florida and California, stability in others, and loss of population estimated in some states. Demand for legal services and for reporter services follows the demographic pattern to a large extent. Estimates show that the number of unfilled reporter positions is in the thousands. Vacancy rates vary from state to state. According to Jean Lea, "We hear from reporting school administrators that students are making job commitments six months before they graduate and that additional job openings are going unfilled" (Lea 1987). The reporter profession faces the reporting needs of a growing nation. Both management and technology will assure that reporting needs are met effectively and efficiently in the future while maintaining a humane approach to reporting. As a result the judiciary, the legal profession and, ultimately, the public will benefit.

Bibliography

Abel, Richard L. "The Transformation of the American Legal Profession," *Law & Society Review*, 20(1986): 7–17.

Abrahams, Henry J. *The Judicial Process*. 5th ed. New York: Oxford University Press, 1986.

Aikman, Alexander B. "Measuring Court Reporter Income and Productivity," *State Court Journal*, 3, no. 16 (Winter 1979), Williamsburg, Va: National Center for State Courts.

Andrews, Lori B. *Birth of a Salesman—Lawyer Advertising and Solicitation*. Chicago: ABA Press, 1979.

Bates Case. See United States Supreme Court.

Benowitz, H. Allen. "An Introduction to Litigation Support," *National Shorthand Reporter*, January 1986, 35–36.

Block, Martin H. "Facing the Challenge," *National Shorthand Reporter*, March 1984, 31–32.

Block, Martin H. "Real-Time Reporting as a Career," *National Shorthand Reporter*, February 1987, 20–21.

Block, Martin H., Ann M. Farrey, Karen S. Jacoby, Cathy Logan, Denise Loser, and Mary E. Smith-Agren. *Reporter Technology: A Basic Text for Instructors and Students Covering Computer-Aided Transcription, Word Processing and Videotape*. Vienna, Va.: National Association of Shorthand Reporters, 1986.

Borgmann, Doreen C. "Justice Prevails," *National Shorthand Reporter*, February 1986, 30.

Brooks, Lynn. "My CAT is No Dog," *National Shorthand Reporter*, March 1985, 24–25.

Carr-Saunders, A. M., and P. A. Wilson. *The Professions*. Oxford, England: Oxford University Press, 1933.

Chomsky, Noam. *Knowledge of Language: Its Nature, Origin, and Use*. New York: Praeger Publishers, 1986.

Church, Thomas, Jr. *Justice Delayed, The Pace of Litigation in Urban Trial Courts.* Williamsburg, Va.: National Center for State Courts, 1978.

Clarke, Arthur C. *Arthur C. Clarke's July 20, 2019, Life in the 21st Century.* New York: Macmillan Publishing Company, 1986.

Cramer, Gary M. "CAT Comes to Sacramento," *National Shorthand Reporter*, May 1984, 32.

Creedy, Richard F. *Time is Money.* New York: E. P. Dutton, 1980.

Cullen, John B. *The Structure of Professionalism. A Qualitative Examination.* New York: Petrocelli Book, 1978.

Curran, Barbara A. "American Lawyers in the 1980s: A Profession in Transition," *Law & Society* Review 20(1986): 19–52.

Delaplain, Richard W. *Computer-Aided Transcription in the Courts.* Williamsburg, Va.: National Center for State Courts, 1981.

Dreyfus, Hubert L. *What Computers Can't Do: The Limits of Artificial Intelligence*, Rev. Ed. New York: Harper & Row, 1979.

Dreyfus, Hubert L., and Stuart E. Dreyfus. *Mind Over Machine: The Power of Human Intuition and Expertise in the Era of the Computer.* New York: Free Press, 1986.

Drill, Denise. "I'm Pro-ProCAT," *National Shorthand Reporter*, August 1985, 27.

Dunlap, James C. See Frost, Sidney W.

Dunn, Linda, and Randy Dunn. "Thanks For the Time, CAT," *National Shorthand Reporter*, March 1984, 30–31.

Ebersole, J. L. *Improving Court Reporting Services.* Washington, D.C.: Federal Judicial Center, 1972.

Etzioni, Amitai (Ed.). *The Semi-Professions and Their Organizations: Teachers, Nurses, Social Workers.* New York: Free Press, 1969.

Farrey, Ann M. See Block, Martin H.

Foderaro, Lisa W. "Teaching Computers to Hear," New York Times, March 23, 1986.

Foster, Harry J. "A Look at InterSteno and our Connection With It." *National Shorthand Reporter*, December 1981, 36–38.

Frost, Sidney W. and James C. Dunlap. *Automated Law Office Systems: A Survey of Today's Tools and Techniques.* St. Paul, Minn.: West Publishing Co., 1983.

Fuller, Lon L. *The Principles of Social Order.* Durham, N.C.: Duke University Press, 1981.

Galleqos, Jan. "A View From the Inside," *National Shorthand Reporter.* December, 1986, 37.

Gilman, Mary Louise. "We're Entitled To Be Paid," *National Shorthand Reporter*, December 1984, 28–31.

Goleman, Daniel. "When the Boss Is Unbearable," *New York Times*, December 28, 1986.

Gosden, Freeman F., Jr. *Direct Marketing Success.* New York: John Wiley & Sons, 1985.

Graham, Michael H. "Nonstenographic Recording of Depositions; The Empty Promise of Federal Rule 30(b)(4)," *Northwestern University Law Review* 72 (1977): 566–594.

Granger, Joan. "Watching the CAT Grow," *National Shorthand Reporter*, December 1984, 26.

Greenwood, J. Michael. *Computer-Aided Transcription: A Survey of Federal Court Reporters' Perceptions*. Washington, D.C.: Federal Judicial Center, 1981.

Greenwood, J. Michael, and Douglas C. Dodge. *Management of Court Reporting Services*. Williamsburg, Va.: National Center for State Courts, 1976.

Greenwood, J. Michael, Julie Horney, M. Daniel Jacoubovitch, Frances B. Lowenstein, and Russell R. Wheeler. *A Comparative Evaluation of Stenographic and Audiotape Methods for United States District Court Reporting*. Washington, D.C.: Federal Judicial Center, 1983.

Greenwood, J. Michael, and Jerry R. Tollar. *User's Guidebook to Computer-Aided Transcription*. Williamsburg, Va.: National Center for State Courts, 1977.

Gross, Ervin G. "Certified Managing Reporters Prepare for Action," *National Shorthand Reporter*, June 1986, 28.

Gross, Ervin G., and Marshall Jorpeland. "The Future of Shorthand Reporting," *National Shorthand Reporter*, May 1984, 16–21.

Halliday, Terence C. "Six Score Years and Ten: Demographic Transitions in the American Legal Profession, 1850–1980," *Law & Society Review*, 20 (1986): 53–78.

Hampden-Turner, Charles. *Maps of the Mind*. New York: MacMillan Publishing Co., 1981.

Hazard, Geoffrey C., Jr., Russell G. Pearce, and Jeffrey W. Stempel. "Why Lawyers Should be Allowed to Advertise: A Market Analysis of Legal Services," *New York University Law Review* 58 (November 1983): 1984–1113.

Henry, Donald L. *The Profitable Professional Practice*. Englewood Cliffs, N.J.: Prentice-Hall, 1985.

Howell, Kay "CAT: Surviving the First Difficult Days," *National Shorthand Reporter*, July 1985, 24–26.

Howell, Kay. "CAT: Hit or Myth?" *National Shorthand Reporter*, July 1986, 26.

Hunt, Kevin R. "Do You Need Text Processor?" *National Shorthand Reporter*, December 1986, 27–32.

Hyatt, Eileen. "Managing a Growing Reporting Firm," *National Shorthand Reporter*, May 1986, 16–18.

Jacoby, Karen S. See Block, Martin H.

Johnson, Larry G. "Using the Court Reporter's Electronic Transcript," *National Shorthand Reporter*, January 1986, 37.

Jorpeland, Marshall. "CAT Comes to Berks County, Pa.," *National Shorthand Reporter*, February 1984, 24–25.

Jorpeland, Marshall. "Writing for Real Time," *National Shorthand Reporter*, February 1986, 25.

Jorpeland, Marshall. See Gross, Ervin G.

Kennedy, Lori O. See Taylor, Regis.

Klink, Sandra. "Helping a Judge Hear with His Eyes," *National Shorthand Reporter*, July 1984, 36–37.

Knapp, Mary H. *The Complete Court Reporter's Handbook*. New York: John Wiley & Sons, 1984.

Kotler, Philip. *Marketing For Nonprofit Organizations*. Englewood Cliffs, N.J.: Prentice-Hall, 1982.

Kotzan, Bruce A. *Court Reporting Practices Among the State Court Systems, Survey*

Results. Williamsburg, Va.: Conference of State Court Administrators, National Center for State Courts, June 1984.

Kramer, Samuel Noah. *History Begins at Sumer*. Garden City, N.Y.: Doubleday & Co., 1959.

Larson, Magali S. *The Rise of Professionalism. A Sociological Analysis*. Berkeley, Calif.: University of California Press, 1977.

Lea, Jean L. "On the Move at BART," *National Shorthand Reporter*, January 1987, 26.

Liles, Bruce L. *An Introduction to Linguistics*. Englewood Cliffs, N.J.: Prentice-Hall, 1975.

Loden, Marilyn. *Feminine Leadership, or How to Succeed in Business Without Being One of the Boys*. New York: Times Books, Random House, 1985.

Logan, Cathy. See Block, Martin H.

Loser, Denise. See Block, Martin H.

Louisell, David W., and Maynard E. Pirsig. "The Significance of Verbatim Recording of Proceedings in American Adjudication," *Minnesota Law Review* 38 (1953): 29–45.

Lynn, Kenneth S. (Ed.). *The Professions in America*. Boston, Mass.: Houghton Mifflin, 1965.

Mann, Emily. *Basics of Legal Procedure for Court Reporters*. Vienna, Va.: National Shorthand Reporters Association, 1980.

Marcus, Bruce W. *Competing for Clients*. Chicago: Probus Publishing Co., 1986.

Meltzer, Curtis A. See Rust, Ronald A.

Meacham, L. Ralph. Memorandum of March 25, 1986 on Report of Evaluation of the Electronic Sound Recording Program in Use by District Court Judges. Washington, D.C.: Administrative Office of the U. S. Courts, 1986.

Miller, Jerome E. "Can Reporters Manage Themselves?" *National Shorthand Reporter*, January 1983, 19–20.

Miner, John B. *People Problems, The Executive Answer Book*. New York: Random House, 1985.

Miner, John B. *Theories of Organizational Behavior*. Hinsdale, Il.: The Dryden Press, 1980.

Mintzberg, Henry. *The Structuring of Organizations*. Englewood Cliffs, N.J.: Prentice-Hall, 1979.

Moore, Perry. *Public Personnel Management—A Contingency Approach*. Lexington, Mass.: Lexington Books, D. C. Heath & Co., 1985.

Moore Wilbert E. *The Professions: Roles and Roles*. New York: Russell Sage Foundation, 1970.

Morphy, Anthony N. *How to Be a Court Reporter*. Bayonne, N.J.: The Pengad Companies, 1980.

Moss, Frederick C. "The Ethics of Law Practice Marketing," *Notre Dame Law Review* 61 (1986): 601–695.

Murphy, Caryle. "The Professional Listening Crew," *The Washington Post*, July 5, 1986.

National Bureau of Standards. *A Study of Court Reporting Systems* (4 vols.). Gaithersburg, Md.: National Bureau of Standards, 1971.

National Center for State Courts. "Court Records: Two Innovative Approaches,"

Report 13, No. 6. Williamsburg, Va.: National Center for State Courts, June 1986.

National Center For State Courts. *Court Reporting Alternatives for Connecticut.* Williamsburg, Va.: National Center for State Courts, 1979.

National Center for State Courts. *An Evaluation of Kentucky's Innovative Approach to Making A Videotope Record of Trial Court Proceedings.* Williamsburg, Va.: National Center for State Courts, 1985.

National Center for State Courts. *An Appraisal of Electronic Centralized Recording System in the Circuit Court for Montgomery County, Maryland.* Williamsburg, VA.: National Center for State Courts, 1986.

National Center for State Courts. *Word Processing in the Courts.* Williamsburg, Va.: National Center for State Courts, 1984.

National Shorthand Reporter. "Our New Code of Professional Conduct," Vienna, Va.: National Shorthand Reporter Association, August 1986, 54–56.

National Shorthand Reporter (Editorial). "The Certified Managing Reporter," *National Shorthand Reporter*, March 1982, 22–25.

National Shorthand Reporters Association. *Celebrating Our Heritage.* Vienna, Va.: National Shorthand Reporters Association, 1976.

National Shorthand Reporters Association. *CAT Needs Assessment: Buying the Right CAT for You.* Vienna, Va.: Committee on CAT, National Shorthand Reporters Association, 1985.

National Shorthand Reporters Association. *1986–1987 NSRA Membership Directory and Registry of Professional Reporters.* Vienna, Va.: National Shorthand Reporters Association, 1986.

Nejelski, Paul, and Russell R. Wheeler. *Widespread Conference on Contemporary and Future Issues in the Field of Court Management.* Racine, Wisc.: The Foundation, 1980.

Nelson, Frank O. *Reducing Transcript Delay: A Guide to Reporter Productivity.* Vienna, Va.: Production Guidelines Task Force, National Shorthand Reporters Association, 1983.

Nelson, Frank O. "CAT on the Feather River Is a Butte," *National Shorthand Reporter*, April 1984, 30–32.

Nelson, Frank O. "The Solo Practitioner," *National Shorthand Reporter*, January 1984, 20–23.

Office of State Courts Administrator (Florida). *Management Guidelines for the CAT Pilot Programs.* Tallahassee, Fla.: Office of State Courts Administrator, State of Florida, 1986.

Pava, Calvin, H. P. *Managing New Office Technology, an Organizational Strategy.* New York: The Free Press, 1983.

Pearce, Russell G. See Hazard, Geoffrey C., Jr.

Pfeffer, Jeffrey and Gerald R. Salancik. *The External Control of Organizations.* New York: Harper & Row, 1978.

Perry, Cindy L. (Ed.). *National Survey of Official Court Reporting.* Vienna, Va.: National Shorthand Reporters Association, 1982.

Perry, Cindy L. (Ed.). *National Survey of Official Court Reporting.* Vienna, Va.: National Shorthand Reporters Association, 1986.

Pirsig, Maynard E. See Louisell, David W.

Praino, Barbara. "Just One Step Forward," *National Shorthand Reporter*, July 1986, 27.

Public Administration Service. *A Study of Shorthand Reporter Transcript Production Costs.* Vienna, Va.: National Shorthand Reporters Association, 1982.

Resource Planning Corp. *A Financial Analysis of Electronic Reporting in Alaska.* Washington, D.C., Resource Planning Corp., 1978.

Restak, Richard M. *The Brain.* New York: Bantam Books, 1984.

Rogers, Everett M. *Diffusion of Innovations* (3rd ed.) New York: Free Press, 1983.

Rogner, Benjamin M. "Do Not Read This Unless . . . ," *National Shorthand Reporter*, June 1984, 30–31.

Rogner, Benjamin M. "When Less Is More," *National Shorthand Reporter*, July 1984, 30–31.

Rogner, Benjamin M. "Recovering Past-Due Receivables," *National Shorthand Reporter*, March 1985, 26–27.

Rogner, Benjamin M. "The Courtroom of the Future," (Detroit) *National Shorthand Reporter*, May 1985, 18–19.

Rogner, Benjamin M. "What to Do Until Help Arrives," *National Shorthand Reporter*, July 1985, 27–28.

Runfola, Thomas F. "CAT Takes a Stand in Maryland, CAT v ER," *National Shorthand Reporter*, May 1984, 22–29.

Runfola, Thomas F. "The Big Picture," *National Shorthand Reporter*, January 1986, 7–8.

Russell, James. *Explaining Mental Life, Some Philosophical Issues in Psychology.* London: Macmillan Press, 1984.

Rust, Ronald A., and Curtis A. Meltzer. "Automated Litigation Support—Westmoreland Libel Case," *National Shorthand Reporter*, July 1986, 34.

Ruthberg, Miles N., and Ernest H. Short. *Administration of Court Reporting in the State Courts.* Williamsburg, Va.: National Center for State Courts, 1973.

Saari, David J. *American Court Management.* Westport, Conn.: Greenwood Press, 1982.

Salancik, Gerald R. See Pfeffer, Jeffrey.

Sanchez, Merilyn. "The Maricopa County CAT Experiment Revisited," *National Shorthand Reporter*, July 1984, 33–35.

Sanchez, Merilyn. *CAT Management for the Official Reporter and Court Administrator.* Vienna, Va.: National Shorthand Reporters Association, 1984.

Sanchez, Merilyn. "CAT in the Courts—Patterns of Ownership," *National Shorthand Reporter*, December 1986, 33–34.

Sayles, Leonard R. *Leadership—What Effective Managers Really Do . . . and How They Do It.* New York: McGraw-Hill Book Co., 1979.

Sayles, Leonard R. "Professionalism, the Key to Big Personal Growth," *Boardroom Reports*, June 1, 1985, 9–10.

Schleich, Laura M. *CAT vs ER, The State of the Art of the Technology and the Debate.* Vienna, Va.: National Shorthand Reporters Association, 1985.

Schleich, Laura M. "CAT News from the Convention," *National Shorthand Reporter*, November 1985, 37–39.

Schleich, Laura M. "CAT Dictionary Conversions," *National Shorthand Reporter*, July 1986, 36–37.

Schlesinger, Arthur M., Jr. "The Challenge of Change," *The New York Times Magazine*, July 27, 1986, 20–21.

Scott, W. Richard. *Organizations—Rational, Natural and Open Systems*. Englewood Cliffs, N.J.: Prentice-Hall, 1981 and 1987 editions.

Short, Ernest H. See Ruthberg, Miles M.

Singer, Cathy. "Guinea Pig for CAT: My Life As a Beta Tester," *National Shorthand Reporter*, December 1984, 27.

Smith-Agren, Mary E. See Block, Martin H.

Stempel, Jeffrey W. See Hazard, Geoffrey C., Jr.

Stout, Ronald. "Planning for Unified Court Budgeting," *Judicature*, 69 (December-January 1986): 205–213.

Suddreth, Jay E. "Managing Change in a World Resistant to Change," *National Shorthand Reporter*, December 1986, 9.

Summers, Robert S. *Lon L. Fuller*. Stanford, Calif.: Stanford University Press, 1984.

Suplee, Curt. "Is This Machine Thinking, Or Not?" *Washington Post*, October 5, 1986, p. C–3.

Taylor, A. "To Copy What Is Right and True; Or the Liability of the Official Reporter Who Does Not," *Kentucky Law Journal* 62 (1973–1974): 964–697.

Taylor, Regis, and Lori O. Kennedy. "The CMR Institute—A Cut Above Excellence," *National Shorthand Reporter*, August 1986, 35.

United States Government Accounting Office. *Federal Court Reporting System: Outdated and Loosely Supervised*. Washington, D.C.: Covernment Accounting Office, 1982.

United States Supreme Court. *Bates v. State Bar of Arizona*. 433 U. S. 350, 1977.

Vollmer, H. M. and D. Mills. *Professionalization*. Englewood Cliffs, N.J.: Prentice-Hall, 1966.

Walker, Anne G. *From Oral to Written: The "Verbatim" Transcription of Legal Proceedings* (2 vols.), Ph.D. diss., Ann Arbor, Mich.: University Microfilms International, 1985.

Walker, Anne G. "The Verbatim Record: The Myth and the Reality," *Discourse and Institutional Authority: Medicine, Education and Law*. Susan Fisher and Alexandra Todd, eds., Norwood, N.J.: Ablex, 1986, 205–222.

Walker, Anne G. "Context Transcripts and Appellate Readers," *Justice Quarterly* 3(1986): 409–428.

Waltz, J. R., and J. Kaplan. *Evidence: Making the Record*. Mineola, NY: Foundation Press, 1982.

Wheeler, Russell R. See Nejelski, Paul.

Wilensky, H. L. "The Professionalization of Everyone?" *American Journal of Sociology* 70(1964): 137–158.

Wilson, Aubrey. *Practice Development for Professional Firms*. London: McGraw-Hill Book Co. (UK) Limited, 1984.

Wilson, Jill Berman. "It Takes More Than a Computer," *National Shorthand Reporter*, May 1984, 30–31.

Wilson, Jill Berman. "A Small CAT May Be Purr-fect for You!" *National Shorthand Reporter*, July 1984, 27–29.

Wilson, Jill Berman. "CAT News from the Convention," *National Shorthand Reporter*, November 1984, 46–47.

Wilson, Jill Berman. "What Will CAT Cost Me?" *National Shorthand Reporter*, July 1985, 20–23.

Wilson, Jill Berman. "Federal Courtrooms Become Communication Centers," *National Shorthand Reporter*, July 1986, 30–31.

Wilson, Jill Berman. "A Management Experiment: The New Mexico Pilot Project," *National Shorthand Reporter*, December 1986, 35–37.

Name Index

Subject Index

About the Author

DAVID J. SAARI is Professor of Judicial Administration at the American University in Washington, D.C. He has served as a management consultant, trial court administrator, and has for more than two decades been in the field of court management. He has published extensively in the areas of public policy, criminal justice, and organization theory.